JESUS IN THE GOSPEL OF JOHN

JESUS IN THE GOSPEL OF JOHN

JACOB JERVELL

TRANSLATED BY HARRY T. CLEVEN

AUGSBURG Publishing House • Minneapolis

JESUS IN THE GOSPEL OF JOHN

Original Norwegian edition entitled *Ingen Har Større Kjærlighet . . .: Fra Johannesvangeliets Jesusbilde,* copyright © 1978 University of Oslo Press.

Scripture quotations unless otherwise noted are from the Revised Standard Version of the Bible, copyright 1946, 1952, and 1971 by the Division of Christian Education of the National Council of Churches.

Library of Congress Cataloging in Publication Data

Jervell, Jacob.
  JESUS IN THE GOSPEL OF JOHN.

  Translation of: Ingen har større kjærlighet.
  Bibliography: p. 86
  1. Jesus Christ—Person and offices—History of
doctrines—Early church, ca. 30-600. 2. Bible. N.T.
John—Criticism, interpretation, etc. I. Title.
BT198.J4513 1984   226'.506   84-14547
ISBN 0-8066-2089-7

Manufactured in the U.S.A.   APH 10-3516

1   2   3   4   5   6   7   8   9   0   1   2   3   4   5   6   7   8   9

CONTENTS

PREFACE

A Jesus who is different? That is the impression we are given when we place the gospel of John, the Fourth Gospel, alongside the other three gospels in our Christian Bible. Jesus speaks differently, uses different language, and acts differently in the gospel of John. The Fourth Gospel gives us a unique, original, and concentrated presentation of Jesus as the incarnate expression of divine love as it relates to the world, history, and humankind.

This book is an attempt to shed light on the message of the Fourth Gospel: how it understands God and humans, life and death, in relation to its interpretation of the person Jesus as love personified. Is the Johannine Jesus also the historical Jesus? What was the environment and the historical situation in the life of the Christian church which provided the basis for the understanding of Jesus which we find recorded in the Fourth Gospel?

A work of this size permits only a broad study of the interpretation of Jesus in the Fourth Gospel. Both the choice of material and its format are the result of a series of lectures delivered at The Institute for the History of Ideas at the University of Oslo.

ONE

The Enigmatic Character of the Gospel

The gospel of John is perhaps the most puzzling writing in the entire New Testament. A great amount of research has been done on this gospel, but scholars have been only partially successful in wresting its secrets from it and solving its mysteries. A casual reading of the gospel does not give one the impression that it has any enigmatic qualities at all. One is, in fact, rather led to believe that it is the most accessible of all the gospels, and that it possesses a monumental simplicity. This is, however, an illusory conclusion.

There are several reasons why we mistake the gospel as being simple.

First, the gospel makes use of a rather limited vocabulary when compared to other New Testament writings, though a closer examination reveals that the author purposely gives the same word two and even three meanings.

Secondly, it is difficult to trace any progression of thought through the writing. The gospel, however, may be compared to a fugue in which the main theme is repeated again and again. It is the very same theme, though viewed from different perspectives. By the time we get to Chapter 20 (not Chapter 21, which is a later addition) and look back at what we have read, we see that not much more has been said than what was already told us in Chapter 1. What has happened, however, is that the main theme throughout these chapters has been extensively developed and given depth and dimension. The main theme, which remains the same and to which the author of the gospel constantly returns, is that Jesus is the Son of God, the very revelation of God himself, with all that this implies for the understanding of the nature of God, humankind, and history.

The basic, underlying question throughout the gospel is, actually, how we are to understand God. There is little in the gospel of what we normally consider to be moral directives and guidelines. Whatever other themes there may seem to be, the person of Jesus Christ and the evangelist's testimony concerning him are always paramount.

The gospel consists primarily of discourses of Jesus, discourses which again and again return to the same theme; namely, what is being said about his own person. The main theme of the other gospels, which we call the synoptic Gospels, is the proclamation of the kingdom of God. This theme has been replaced in the Fourth Gospel by the discourses in which Jesus proclaims his mission. All the gospels emerge from the community of faith, the church, and declare that Jesus is the Son of God. They are not, therefore, historical documents as such. The gospel of John, more than any of the others, must be characterized as a gospel of the church.

The literary form given to this writing, which we call gospel, was created within Christendom and is unique to it. There is no parallel to this type of literary form apart from Christian literature. From a literary point of view, *gospel* implies a "historically" construed portrayal of the suffering, death, and resurrection of Jesus, with a detailed preface describing his life and deeds. But we cannot in this connection speak of a historical account according to our understanding of the term. More than the other gospels, it must be recognized that the Fourth Gospel has the character of meditation and conscious theological reflection. We need not read far before realizing how different this gospel is from the others. This is clearly perceptible from the language, to which we have already made reference. Language, in this context, is closely connected to the concepts presented in the writing. In his portrayal of the Christ, it is obvious that John uses different words, expressions, and concepts than the other evangelists. His thought pattern is not the same. We may note the emphasis on contrasts, such as light/dark, lie/truth, love/hate, etc. There are the unique "I am" statements of Jesus which he uses to speak about himself. These are used together with related statements such as "the Light of the world," "the Water of life," "the Bread of life," etc. We are told that Jesus has ascended to heaven and descended from heaven; the relationship between the Father and the Son is discussed at length.

This dissimilarity from the other gospels is also seen in the chronological and the topographical framework of the Fourth Gospel. According to the gospel of Mark, the oldest of the four, Jesus' public ministry lasted a year and his life ended with the journey up to Jerusalem and the crucifixion. John, on the other hand, says Jesus' public ministry lasted three years—that Jesus in fact made several journeys to Jerusalem and was active in Jerusalem the last six months or so of his life.

We note still other differences in his method of presentation. In the synoptic Gospels, the accounts of Jesus' life and teaching are a composite of individual stories and sayings—separate and independent of each other—which only later have been edited into a sort of "biographical" whole. The one exception to this is the passion history which the gospels, from the beginning, have presented in a consecutive order.

The gospel of John, on the other hand, consists primarily of comparatively long, detailed discourses. These, however, are not composites of individual statements originally existing independently of each other. They center around a definite theme often presented in dialog form, giving the gospel a somewhat dramatic quality.

Finally, there is a noticeable difference between the synoptic Gospels and the Fourth Gospel regarding the material itself. John has very little material in common with the first three gospels. The discourses of Jesus in John have no parallels, for the most part, in the other gospels. In addition, even the language used by Jesus is different.

The differences between the synoptic Gospels and the Fourth Gospel give the latter an enigmatic character. This is true not only of the external differences we have touched upon, but also of an internal difference we have not yet discussed, namely, the theology of John.

Before considering the theological content of the Fourth Gospel, let us briefly list some of the problems which confront scholars as they deal with this writing, even if the problems are not as a rule solved with any great degree of satisfaction.

1. We are not able to determine the original form of the gospel. We need not read far in order to realize that the material is not presented in its original sequence, as is evident from a number of striking discrepancies. A good example is John 14:31, seen in relation to Chapters 15 and 16. Jesus, in 14:31, closes his farewell discourse to the disciples with an admonition to them to depart, namely, to the place of suffering. But the farewell discourse then continues in the following chapters. We find a similar situation in comparing 6:1 with 5:1. An obvious disorder has occurred

through the transmission of the material, and it is not possible for us to reconstruct the original sequence.* It is also obvious that the gospel has been reworked after the first writing. The original version ended with Chapter 20, as revealed in verses 30 and 31. Then follows Chapter 21, an early addition, where we are told in verse 24 of a group of people who have added this section to the gospel. The account of the woman taken in adultery, 7:53—8:11, is also a later addition. What we cannot ascertain is the origin of these additions, whether they have come from a group of the evangelist's pupils or from another source.

2. The identity of the author or authors, since it is not at all clear whether there was only one or several, is unknown to us. The original writing from Chapter 20 does not identify the writer for us. The author or authors remain anonymous. Tradition, which in this case may be traced back to ca. A.D. 200, attributes authorship to the apostle John, an eyewitness of the events described. This is untenable, however, for further investigation makes it quite clear that no eyewitness could have written this gospel. Had it been written by an apostle, in this case John, it would be impossible to give a reasonable explanation as to why this gospel only gradually and against definite opposition from a broad section within the church, was able to make a breakthrough and finally gain acceptance. There are, in addition, as already mentioned, indications that, not only one individual, but several, perhaps even a particular school with its own traditions quite independent of the first three gospels and Paul, could be responsible for the writing. The author, in other words, is and remains unknown. Nor do we know where the gospel came into being. On the other

*Trans. note: The disjunction here is geographical. According to 5:1, Jesus is in Jerusalem, but in 6:1 he is crossing the Sea of Galilee far from Jerusalem.

hand, we are able to place its approximate date of origin near the close of the first century A.D., since we have manuscript fragments dating from this period.

3. We cannot even say with certainty for whom the gospel was written—who its readers were and to whom the gospel was addressed. One of our most difficult problems is knowing with clarity the circumstances and the surroundings in which the gospel was written. Widely varying religious movements converge in this writing. There is clear evidence of Jewish biblical knowledge, mysticism, and Jewish sect piety. There are also traces pointing to the influence of the Hellenistic mystery religions and popular philosophy, in addition to Gnosticism. It is difficult to determine whether the gospel was actually written for Christians, Gentiles, or Jews. We can imagine that the author sought to reach a number of dissimilar groups in order to show the importance of the Christian faith for them in spite of their background and environment.

John leaves us, then, with a number of unresolved problems, historical, literary, and religious. To a degree, this is also true of the theology and thought of the gospel.

In spite of all the problems, however, there are a number of things in the gospel which are comprehensible to us. We shall now look at some of these.

We have in the gospel of John the original, independent proclamation of the Christian faith, but this must also be seen against the author's own contemporary interpretation of Christianity. In selecting the gospel literary form to convey his message, and thereby presenting the events connected with Jesus in a historical progression determined by time and place, the writer declares that the events which he describes are historical fact; that they have actually taken place. This is the intention of a statement such as "the Word became flesh," 1:14; the Word did, in fact, become a human being, but the author is not thereby an historian. It is not his purpose to produce a photographic study or a detailed, objective report. As the author writes the story of Jesus, he often interrupts the narrative to discuss the deep significance of the events he portrays. His work must, therefore, be understood as a message of faith and a reinterpretation of the events connected with that faith.

The author is anything but neutral in regard to those events. He is not a spectator to what happens, but is personally involved the whole time. He is even a participant in the events. This is the only way he is able to write history. As far as he is concerned, what he writes is objective history; yet we must emphasize again that, according to our modern concept of history, what he writes is not an objective presentation of the facts.

But the author is willing to stake his life on the truth of what he writes. It is useless for us to apply our sophisticated methods of scientific research as a means of validating the historicity of the events or to determine thereby if these events have in fact occurred or undergone embellishment. To do so would be to misinterpret the intentions of the author. He wants us to be familiar, not only with the events themselves, but also the deeper significance of those events. This is certainly true of the other gospels as well, but not to the same extent as in the Fourth Gospel. Here history and proclamation are insolubly intertwined. What Jesus says throughout the gospel is tinted by the language, style, and form chosen by the author and/or his school. To answer a question raised earlier, the gospel of John does not portray the historical Jesus, but seeks to interpret and understand his significance. Or, to put it another way, it shows us the effects of the work and activity of Jesus. The author states the purpose of the gospel in 20:31: "These (signs) are written that you may believe that Jesus is the

Christ, the Son of God, and that believing you may have life in his name."

The Structure of the Gospel

The gospel begins with a hymnic prolog, 1:1-18, which proclaims that the divine, eternal *Logos* (Word) has become a person in Jesus Christ. He is the only person to reveal God. The first main section of the gospel, 1:19—12:50, portrays the public ministry of Jesus. This is described chiefly as a conflict between Jesus and his own people. Here Jesus appears as the Father's representative, as God's face turned toward the world.

The second main section, Chapters 13–20, records Jesus' return to his divine source of origin, the Father. The first section, which contains the so-called farewell discourses, is played out by Jesus and the disciples. Here the question is raised as to how the gap between the exalted Lord and those who believe in him may be bridged following his departure.

The passion history is recorded in Chapters 18–19 of the second section, even though, strictly speaking, we cannot here really refer to a passion history, for the author of John does not use these events to describe the humiliation of Jesus. Suffering and death, according to the author, only reveal more clearly the divinity of Jesus. Finally, Chapter 20 describes the appearances of the risen one. As already explained, Chapter 21 is a later addition.

This is only a rough outline. What is more important is what really is said. In the gospel of John it is amazing to see how Jesus' humanity has a tendency to disappear. Of course, we do not mean his real humanity, but its presentation, which is quite unlike the other gospels. In portraying Jesus, the author of John shows us a Jesus who is more truly divine than he is truly human, for it is the con-frontation with the divine which permits one to be fully human and not something less, something demonic. But the relationship of the human to the divine is not the real issue. The author of John is not really concerned with the human aspects of the person of Jesus; his interest is in painting a picture of the divine Jesus. We might summarize his opinion in this manner: In Jesus, and Jesus alone, the divine is made audible, visible, and obtainable in the pres-ent. This is the actual theme of the gospel, though it is developed with the use of a number of terms and titles such as *Logos* (the Word), Messiah, Son of man, Son of God, the Son, Savior of the world, etc. Of these, the most important are the titles Son of God and the Son.

TWO

God's Only Son

Christianity has not been alone in speaking about the Son of God. This concept was both widespread and in common usage in the religious setting of early Christianity. We shall take a brief look at the non-Christian use of this term before attempting to see how it has been used in the gospel of John.

In Egypt and among diverse Oriental groups, the king was believed to be divine or the son of the deity. This could be interpreted to mean that he was a direct descendant of the gods. It could also be understood to mean that he was born in a manner unlike other human beings, that he entered the world in a miraculous way. He could also reveal the heavenly and divine. In some periods the title Son of God was used to refer to Hellenistic conquerors and Roman emperors. The title was not only used to mean these, however; in the Hellenistic world it was also ascribed to miracle workers and those capable of revealing divine mysteries, sometimes also called divine men. In addition, it was believed that in the dedicatory rites of the mystery religions one could pass over from the human to the divine. There were many so-called divine men in the Hellenistic world.

The title Son of God is also familiar to us from the Old Testament and later Judaism, but here the term is understood metaphorically. The nation Israel is sometimes referred to as the Son of God, as in Exodus 4:22. Here it does not imply that Israel has descended from God, but has been chosen by God. The term also refers to the king of Israel (2 Sam. 7:14; Ps. 2:7), who became the Son of God not by birth, but by adoption. He is, therefore, the one God has chosen to act in his stead. One question we might raise is the extent to which the Son of God title is used in connection with the Messiah, especially in later Judaism, but our sources give us too little information to answer this question.

By using the Son of God title, the gospel of John took a term familiar to the age, although the term has various shades of meaning. The author of the gospel did not borrow this term from the general religious surroundings, however, but rather as it was already in use in Christian tradition. We see this from the other gospels as well as the writings of Paul. The author of John was not content merely to use the title Son of God as such. He prefers the definite form "the Son" which corresponds to the term "the Father" used about God. This clearly has a polemical purpose, for the title Son of God is to be reserved for Jesus alone. No one else may properly be addressed that way. There is only one Son who is in such a unique relationship to God that this term may be applied to him. The gospel states this by referring to the only Son, that is, the only Son God has. The gospel avoids the commonly accepted picture of God as the father of all humankind or of all believers. We find an exception to this in 20:17. The purpose here is also clear: to speak about God as Father has meaning only in relation to this one person, Jesus. This is to reveal the exclusiveness of his sonship, upon which anyone else's sonship must depend.

As to what the gospel of John means by this term, we note that it does not talk about a divine, miraculous birth in the way that Luke and Matthew describe the virgin birth. The gospel of John does not deny the virgin birth, but the concept is not mentioned in the Fourth Gospel because it is not a divine birth which really makes Jesus the Son of God. Rather, John stresses a thought taken from the Old Testament and late Judaism. Over and over again Jesus refers to himself as the one who is sent. About 50 times the gospel makes use of two Greek verbs which may be translated *send* or *send out*. We could possibly also say *to delegate*. The meaning is that Jesus, as the Son of God, is given God's full authority and represents him in the world.

The background of this idea is juridical rather than mythical, as the term Son of God was generally conceived, and stems from Jewish rather than Hellenistic thought. There is a phrase from the language of Jewish law: "The one sent is as the one who sent him." Thus, it is through the representative, and him alone, that we are connected with the one who sent him. The representative has been given full authority, and he speaks and acts on behalf of the one who has given him a task to perform. To receive and negotiate with the representative is equal to receiving and negotiating with the sender. This in no way diminishes the personhood of the representative or suggests that he mechanically mouths words and opinions which are not his own. The point is, rather, that the representative puts himself totally at the disposal of the one who has given him a task. He gives up his own interests, making the desires and wishes of the one who sent him his own.

In the Fourth Gospel, the term "the Son," must be understood with the foregoing in mind. Jesus seeks to be the voice and arm of the Father. Therefore the Johannine Jesus continually emphasizes the fact that he does not speak his own words, but those of his Father (3:34; 7:16; 8:26,38,40). He does not accomplish his own work, but the Father's (4:34; 5:17,19ff.,30,36). He does not do his own will, but the Father's (4:34; 5:30; 6:38, etc.). It is a misunderstanding to believe that the gospel of John makes Jesus into God, or identical with God. The gospel permits the Jews to bring the accusation of blasphemy against Jesus, that is, that he equates himself with God (5:18). This criticism is pushed aside in the gospel. Jesus is not God but God's representative, and, as such, so completely and totally acts on God's behalf that he stands in God's stead before the world. The gospel clearly states that God and Jesus are not to be understood as identical persons, as in 14:28, "The Father is greater than I." It does not say, "We are one." Rather, we are told in 10:38 and 14:10, "The Father is in me and I am in the Father." This may sound mystical, but it has no relation to mysticism as seen from the background material sketched above. Jesus says, "I am not alone, for the Father is with me" (16:32). Statements like these and their parallels are variations of one and the same thought, namely: Jesus is a man in the presence of God.

What gives this concept of the one who is sent out, the Son, such great importance in the gospel of John is the supposition which determines our understanding of God: "No one has ever seen God" (1:18; 5:37; 6:46). There is no human approach to God. He is the invisible and the unknown. It is impossible to go past the representative directly to the one who sends him. There is no possibility of access to God, or knowledge about him, or fellowship with him apart from that provided by the Son. A crucial statement for our understanding of who Jesus is in the Fourth Gospel occurs in 14:9: "He who has seen me has seen the Father" (see also 1:18).

According to the gospel of John, then, we are being confronted by God himself as we come into contact with the words and deeds of Jesus. It is God who speaks through the words of Jesus. Thus, another characteristic of the gospel of John also becomes clear, namely, that everything Jesus says concerning himself is also a statement about God.

Having said this, the question must also be raised: How does the gospel of John understand God? When Jesus declares, "I am the bread of life" in 6:35 ("I" here signifying the one who gives both life and existence), he is saying that God himself is the bread of life. When it is stated, "I am the light of the world" in 8:12 and 9:5 (that is, the one who gives us the possibility of understanding ourselves and the world) it is really God who is the light of the world. When Jesus characterizes himself as the good shepherd in 10:11 and 17 (that is, the one who offers his life and person for others), it is God who offers himself to and on behalf of humankind. By this it is said that individuals, humankind, historical events, and the outcome of history itself are not subject to a blind fate or impersonal destiny, but are in the hand of a father who loves. Jesus' life is understood as the revelation and personification of God's self-offering, self-sacrificial love for humankind. This is unforgettably manifested in the foot washing account (13:1-17), in which Jesus is depicted as the one who washes the feet of his disciples. This is clearly the duty of a slave, but here it signifies God's self-offering love. This act of humiliation indicates the nature of God, which humanizes people. For that love is the content of the life God has given humankind.

If we adhere to the most essential aspect in properly understanding the identity of the Son—namely, that he is sent and thus is God's face turned toward the world, and that he consequently speaks and acts in absolute dependence on the Father—it becomes apparent that the gospel of John cannot express strongly enough its conviction that Jesus perfectly exercises divine power. This is most clear from the discourse in 5:17ff. Here two divine prerogatives are ascribed to Jesus. One is that he creates or gives life (5:21-26). This reinforces the concept, already mentioned, that Jesus is sent. Because it can also be said that the disciples are sent, it can be said that the spokesman, the Paraclete, is sent. This says, then, that God sends out the Spirit. But the discourse about having the ability to create life is reserved for Jesus alone when it is said that he is sent out. It is the creation of life which distinguishes God as God and creator. John 5:26 states: "For as the Father has life in himself, so he has granted the Son also to have life in himself." The assertion here is that in all existence there is only one, namely God, who has life in himself. All others have life only indirectly, i.e., life which stems from the primary source of life, namely God.

The notion of having life in oneself, Jesus' power to create, is illustrated by the raising of Lazarus (Chapter 11). We are not really dealing with a miracle story here, i.e., an account of the miraculous in the normal understanding of the term. It is rather a demonstration of Jesus' ability and right to create life. This means that God creates life through him by raising the dead. He also gives eternal life through Jesus, something to which we shall return a bit later. The notion that Jesus creates and gives life is developed in the gospel to point back to Jesus' preincarnational existence. This is evident from the prolog (1:3): "All things were made through him."

The second special divine prerogative ascribed to Jesus is expressed in the word "judgment" (Greek, *krisis*). As Lord and ruler, it is up to God to pronounce judgments over the lives and deeds of people. Again we refer to the discourse of 5:17ff, and particularly verse 22, which most clearly states Jesus' authority to judge: "The Father judges no one, but has given all judgment to the Son." This is also the point of verse 27: He "has given him authority to execute judgment," i.e., Jesus determines the fate of humankind. In John's gospel, to give life and to judge are two sides of the same coin. Both describe the same divine activity, namely, what is called the eschatological act of judgment. This requires further clarification. The gospel of John builds upon a commonly held notion of both Judaism and Christianity: the belief that God will place all history and all mankind before his judgment throne at the end of time. History and existence are limited by and held by God. The result of this eschatological judgment will be either acquittal, i.e., eternal life in a new realm, or condemnation.

What is unique in the gospel of John is a new interpretation of the eschatological judgment over history. That judgment day, which is a day totally God's, is the time when each individual will appear before the Son of God. Therefore, judgment day is not a purely future event. It is certainly true that the gospel of John envisions a future judgment at the conclusion of history, as is evident from a number of references, among them 12:48, but the main emphasis in John is that judgment already takes place within time and history (see 5:24ff.; 15:22ff.; *et al.*). It will suffice in this context to say that according to the gospel of John, to be God's Son involves the performance of divine functions in absolute dependence on the Father.

There is also a group of statements related to the language concerning Jesus as the Son of God. The understanding that Jesus performs divine functions stretches the understanding of Jesus as a representative or emissary as far as possible, perhaps even too far. The language is strained. A more precise understanding of the language which refers to Jesus as the Son of God in the gospel of John may be gained by noting the kinds of questions which the evangelist raises: What is Jesus' origin? From whence does he come? (See 7:29ff.; 9:29f.; 19:9.) The answer to these questions is given in mythical but unambiguous language. In spite of Jesus' human existence, says the gospel account, he is an alien in this world. Or perhaps more correctly, he reveals how this world has become alienated from God. Jesus comes from the heavenly realm where life is created. The gospel emphasizes that Jesus comes from "above," (3:31; 8:14,23): "You are from below, I am from above; you are of this world, I am not of this world" (see also 13:3; 16:28; 17:5,24).

We can sum up this understanding by referring to the statements about Jesus' preexistence. These inform us that Jesus existed together with the Father before his life in the world; in fact, before the world was created. Jesus is therefore raised above the prophetic category as one who speaks with full authority from God. Jesus is eternally with God; the mystery of God which Jesus reveals to the world is the eternal unity of the Father and the Son. God is fellowship, God is love, a fact which according to biblical understanding is not based primarily on emotion, but on the will to act in fellowship. This also explains the fact that the gospel of John has no "catechism" and knows only one commandment, namely, the commandment to love. The understanding of Jesus' preexistence is that it reveals the divine authority with which Jesus speaks. The divine reality is made audible, tangible, and visible because Jesus reveals its essence to history and the world. He thereby also reveals human reality in that he shows the world from whence it has come and the context in which it properly belongs.

The *consequences* of this knowledge are readily discernible. The moment Jesus describes himself as the only one who has seen the Father and as the only one who is "from above," it is impossible for people to criticize or dispute these claims. It is as though a red thread runs through the gospel, namely, that Jesus is continually suffering rejection and being accused of blasphemy. Here, as in the other gospels, the accusations against him come primarily from religious circles. His enemies have their own criteria as to how the Son of God and the Messiah should appear and act. Jesus does not fit their expectations. For them, the Messiah should be represented by a mighty politico-religious conqueror who defends and liberates the chosen. Jesus, however, exemplifies a distinct piety; his human origin is unknown. Jesus himself breaks with an important legal aspect which had validity also in the area of religion, namely, that no one may stand forth and defend his own case (5:34ff.; 8:13ff.). Jesus asserts that there is no human testimony or premises which can legitimize who he is. These have no significance or value for him. Jesus alone knows who and what he is. There are no religious yardsticks by which to measure him; if there were, there are those who would use them to entrench themselves in a kind of self-adequacy.

Perhaps we can make this clearer in another way. It is Jesus' origin which give his words their validity. According to the gospel, Jesus' origin is not determined by a specific historical situation or a specific human experience. His words have neither been determined by the needs and requirements of the moment, nor are they the outgrowth of human religious emotions or piety. They are not a product of history—it is rather his words which have created a

new historical situation. The words are not to be scruti-
nized; it is rather those who hear them who are under
scrutiny. The hearer cannot subject the words to criticism;
the words place the hearer under criticism. This must be
understood in relation to the gospel of John's understanding
of the Word of God. God's Word is absolute and therefore
not subject to human evaluation. God's Word requires only
one thing, and that is a response of faith on the part of the
hearer. Faith in the gospel of John is not adherence to
theses and dogmas, but is the submission of one's life and
being to "the truth" which Jesus represents. This truth, in
the Fourth Gospel, is best translated "reality," which is the
direct opposite of illusion.

Jesus' contemporaries discredit his claims and statements
as blasphemous and false. The rejected Jesus cannot enter
into their discussion. He labels the rejection of his opponents as sin, which in the Fourth Gospel is much more
serious than the transgression of moral law: it is the rejection
of truth and reality. This implies, then, that one lives in
rebellion against one's maker, who has chosen to disclose
himself in Jesus of Nazareth. As a result, the source of one's
own origin is denied and one lives in a state of self-decep-
tion. The prolog to the gospel (1:1-18), which speaks about
the divine Word or Logos, the source of all human life and
understanding, personified in Jesus Christ, must be understood in this light. Apart from him, the divine Word does
not exist. Sin in the Fourth Gospel is therefore to believe
a lie about one's self because one believes a lie about God.
The truth is found, rather, in faith. We must understand
that, in the gospel of John, faith is closely connected with
the Johannine concept of God, i.e., God as love rather than
something abstract and theoretical. Thus, a relationship
with God is possible only through a personal relationship
of unconditional love. Real love does not impose conditions

but gives freely of itself without reservations and restrictions. Only in this context is love really love. This is true, *mutatis mutandis*, in the gospel of John. It is in the yielding of oneself that one truly becomes human. Only in relation to God is one given the possibility of self-understanding, and this happens only through the revelation of the divine through the one who speaks with divine authority.

THREE

The World in Crisis

We shall proceed to the theme of judgment, which, in reality, simply adds depth to the gospel's portrayal of Jesus as the revealer of divine truth.

Belief in the divine judgment of humankind at the end of time is a notion common to both Judaism and early Christianity. We must understand, however, that the emphasis here was not primarily on judgment of the individual nor judgment which occurred at the moment of death. It is humankind as a whole which shall be subject to God's final act of judgment. This understanding of judgment is closely connected to the view of history as something limited by time. The all-encompassing act of judgment in the last days marks the termination of history and the beginning of a new world order, "the kingdom of God."

The day of judgment has both negative and positive aspects. On the negative side is the obliteration of all unrighteousness, acts of tyranny, and oppression, but with the positive result that God will then establish righteousness and mercy. The resurrection signifies the fulfillment of this righteousness. The great eschatological act of judgment is the decisive, final, and conclusive revelation of God, the moment when God reveals that he is indeed God. This Jewish concept was carried over into early Christianity, which interpreted Jesus to signify the beginning of the end. That is to say, in him the process was set into motion which was to end soon with the determinative act of judgment and the conclusion of history.

It became evident to the early Christians that the final kingdom had not yet arrived with the advent of Jesus. This led to the belief that the final conclusion of history would come with the second coming of Christ. Thus, Jesus would return again. This is most evident from the so-called apocalyptic literature. The writer of John is familiar with the many thoughts about the day of judgment then prevailing, but adds his own unique interpretation. The gospel of John does away almost completely with apocalyptic language. Its uniqueness with regard to judgment is that judgment is not only regarded as a future event, but it is also something which takes place in the present. It happens not at some random moment in a person's life, but at a time determined by the moment of confrontation with the one who makes God known. The emphasis upon Christ as the only one who reveals God means that in him history has arrived at its goal and destination. Jesus is not a turning point in history, but an end point. Thus, a new revelation of God sometime in the future, with new and heretofore unknown aspects of his nature being disclosed, will not happen. The future will not bring anything significantly new because what is important has already been revealed. In Christ, humanity has been brought before the final reality and therefore also into judgment.

We find a number of statements in the gospel of John which reflect earlier descriptions of events having to do with the last days. But the evangelist brings all this into the present as one is confronted with Christ; it is this which is the moment of judgment: "Truly, truly, I say to you, he who hears my word and believes him who sent me, has eternal life; he does not come into judgment, but has passed from death to life. Truly, truly, I say to you, the hour is coming and now is, when the dead shall hear the voice of the Son of God, and those who hear will live. For as the Father has life in himself, so he has granted the Son also to have life in himself, and has given him authority to execute judgment, because he is the Son of man" (5:24-27). "He who believes in him is not condemned; he who does not believe is condemned already, because he has not believed in the name of the only Son of God. And this is the judgment, that the light has come into the world, and men loved darkness rather than light, because their deeds were evil" (3:18-19). At the same time, we must be aware of the fact that the Fourth Gospel has not dismissed every thought of a future day of judgment or an eternal life yet to come. These aspects are present, but a present judgment and eternal life which begins now are essential characteristics of the Fourth Gospel.

The passages we have cited appear to contain an element of contradiction. On the one hand, Jesus states that he has not come to judge the world (3:17; 8:15; 12:47). Rather, he has come in order to save, to give life in God. On the other hand, references such as 3:19; 5:22,27; 8:16; 9:39; and 12:48 clearly indicate that part of Jesus' activity is precisely that of being a judge. This apparent contradiction, however, is in reality no contradiction at all. There only seems to be such on the surface. We have earlier indicated that the author of the Fourth Gospel plays on the double meaning of words. The Greek word for "judgment" used in the gospel may mean two things: (1) to separate, segregate, or keep apart, and (2) to pronounce judgment, which, in a negative sense, means to condemn. The statements which declare that Jesus' purpose in coming is not to bring judgment upon the world clearly indicate that his purpose or intention is not to bring condemnation. In making this assertion, the evangelist reveals a certain polemical stance on his part in his understanding of Christ as judge, reacting against the idea of a negative and destructive activity by which God takes revenge upon his enemies. The gospel certainly adheres to the inevitability of judgment over humankind in relation to Christ, but this does not bear the stamp of being condemnatory. It is rather judgment in the sense of being divided or separated.

The first reference in the gospel to treat this matter is 3:19-21: "And this is the judgment, that the light has come into the world, and men loved darkness rather than light, because their deeds were evil. For every one who does evil hates the light, and does not come to the light, lest his deeds should be exposed. But he who does what is true comes to the light, that it may be clearly seen that his deeds have been wrought in God." The word *light* is an often used term in the gospel of John which signifies "divine reality" or "ultimate reality." The metaphorical language is simple enough: One sees nothing in the dark. Only with the assistance of light are we able to distinguish ourselves and our surroundings. The gospel of John utilizes this language to show that human existence becomes clear only in light of the divine.

The light referred to in the gospel is the light connected to the person of Jesus, as expressed by Jesus himself: "I am the light of the world" (8:12). This is to say, Jesus is representative of the divine reality which alone explains the significance of human existence. At the same time, this enables us to understand the meaning of the term *judgment*.

Jesus, as the manifestation of the divine reality or light, automatically brings about a separation or judgment between those who are in the light and those who are not. Because the light confronts a person with ultimate reality, that person is faced with a crisis. The absolute division between good and evil, truth and falsehood, reality and illusion, is manifested in the appearance of Jesus. Dependent upon one's response to the divine revelation in Jesus, one pronounces judgment upon oneself: "And this is the judgment, that the light has come into the world, and men loved darkness rather than light" (3:19). This indicates that the light is hated and avoided so as not to reveal what one really is. The word *hate* in New Testament thought does not so much express an emotional feeling as it does an action, that is, the action of cutting oneself off, of holding oneself separate and apart. The expression "to hate one's enemy" means to separate oneself from that person. "To love one's enemy," on the other hand, means to have fellowship with the enemy, clearly a contradiction of terms, for the moment one loves the enemy one obviously has fellowship with that person, and as a consequence that person is no longer an enemy! The judgment which takes place with the coming of Jesus is, therefore, in the Fourth Gospel, the decision made by the individual by which one pronounces judgment upon oneself, i.e., one separates oneself from truth and chooses falsehood instead. This judgment is upheld by God.

It is important for us to note here that judgment is not made on the basis of one's relationship to moral norms, but rather on that which forms the basis for these, namely, one's relationship to divine reality. The decisive factor represented by the day of judgment in the gospel of John is, therefore, the fact that humankind is confronted with Jesus as the Son of God. The gospel is, at the same time, quite familiar with traditional Christian thought which affirms a final day of judgment at the end of time. We have references to this day of judgment in several passages, among them 5:25 and 12:47ff. But it must be emphasized once again that this day is only a confirmation of what has already taken place in a person's life with regard to one's relationship to Christ as the final revelation of God, for it shall be disclosed on that day that in Christ history had already arrived at its destination.

The evangelist's discussion of the coming of Jesus as an act of judgment reaches its climax in the account concerning his death. Judgment in this context receives its most paradoxical form, as may be seen from the unique presentation the passion story receives in the Fourth Gospel. Perhaps it is incorrect to speak about a passion story in John at all, because this gospel does not present Jesus as a suffering victim, but rather as the one who himself acts throughout this whole narrative. It is Jesus who takes the initiative at the time of his arrest, 18:1. It is Jesus who, during his trials before the chief priest and Pilate, guides the interrogations and is on top of the situation, 18:12ff., 28ff. It is Jesus who determines the time of his death, and who dies fully conscious that his work has been accomplished, 19:28ff. Seen only on the surface, the conflict between Jesus and the Jewish people ends with his apparent defeat. They have condemned him to death. But the author emphasizes that they could accomplish this only with the help of false information and accusations brought to the Roman authorities. According to the author, it is rather his opponents who are condemned and who suffer defeat. In the proceedings against Jesus, the divine revelation reaches a climax in Jesus' willingness to become the sacrifice and in his love voluntarily given. This unselfish willingness to sacrifice himself is the ultimate expression of God's nature, which is to love (see 3:16 and 1 John 4:8). It is in rejecting this divine love revealed in the person of Jesus—and at that with the help of lies—that the attempt is made to take God's life, i.e., by destroying his only representative. In rejecting Jesus, they only bring judgment upon themselves. The victor is the seemingly conquered one. The judges are those who are condemned. Jesus can therefore validly characterize his death as the final judgment upon the world, as in 12:31: "Now is the judgment of this world." Jesus' demand that he be acknowledged as God's Son and his authority to act on God's behalf are legitimate and right according to the gospel. His demand is a demonstration of his act of love, confirmed by his resurrection which signifies his exaltation to a divine position of dominance. The accusations brought against him by his adversaries are groundless, as is demonstrated by their hatred and lies.

FOUR

History and the
Christ of History

At this point it may be helpful for us to make some observations about the Fourth Gospel's understanding of history. We must first note that the author is no historian or philosopher in the sense of seeking to reconstruct the past or to determine various causes and effects within the historical process. In his understanding of the past he is far removed from our own modern methods of historical-critical research. But he does have a definite understanding of history which is certainly colored by his interpretation of the Christ. The theme of history, according to the gospel of John, is the conflict between darkness and the light, truth and falsehood, or reality and illusion. Summarily this concerns itself with the conflict between God and the world. The conflict came into being as the result of humankind's self-assertive rebelliousness against God. We are guilty of denying God as our source of origin and taking our life and existence for granted. The world or cosmos, understood as collective humankind, is not an evil entity in itself, but becomes so the moment we deny our origin and place ourselves above our creator. Humankind subsequently falls into two major categories. On the one hand, those who are of the truth and do the truth (the word "do" is important because one's nature and character is revealed in one's deeds), and on the other hand, those who are of the world and do evil, those who deal in lies (8:23,44,47; 10:26-27; 17:6,9,14; 18:37). Until Christ's coming these two groups are intermingled. Until then the conflict between God and the world is latent and hidden. There is no knowledge of any progression forward toward an acknowledgment of God. This is the first phase of history.

A second and critical phase of history is the coming of Christ, for it is in this event that the rift between God and the world becomes an open conflict, described in Chapters 1–12 in several clashes between Jesus and the Jews. We are to understand the irony in the claim made by the Jews that they are the chosen people of God, when in fact the gospel says they are the representatives of the world which lives in enmity with God. Thus the religious conflict depicted in John is neither localized nor limited by time. The conflict, which is described as taking place in a definite geographical setting or time framework, only indicates a larger event in which humankind as a whole is implicated. What is really being dealt with here is the conflict between God and the whole world. Jesus is God's representative in this conflict who in revealing the Father simultaneously shows us who we are, our origin and our destination. This also helps explain, in part, why the gospel of John is little concerned with explaining the nature of God. It is not the nature of God which is in need of definition, but that of humankind. Therefore, the Jews stand in this conflict on the opposing side as representatives of the world, i.e., humankind opposed to God. In their rejection of Jesus, the Jews reveal that they live in open conflict with God himself. They will not acknowledge their dependence upon him,

but use their religion to defend themselves against him.
The revelation of the Father is therefore also the disclosure
of humanity's lie about itself.

Again it is the coming of Jesus which determines the
conflict, the actual theme of history. It does so in the first
place, because these two groups of people—those who are
of the truth and those who are not—are separated from
each other by their response to Christ. It is the church,
according to the gospel, which is representative of the group
which "is of the truth," those who acknowledge God's supreme authority and their own human limitations. In the
second place, the conflict is brought to a head (it remains
unresolved and no agreement is reached) in the proceedings
against Jesus which result in his suffering and death. As
indicated earlier, the passion story is here understood as a
process in which the apparent victors become the losers.
Upon their heads the guilty sentence is pronounced by none
other than God himself, for he alone wields power and
authority. For the gospel writer, the resurrection is the sign
of Jesus' victory and exaltation. His return to the Father
seals the fate and destiny of humankind. Thus, according
to the Fourth Gospel, a historical event has once and for
all pronounced the verdict upon all falsehood and all opposition to God.

The third phase of history is the post-Jesus age or the
period of the church. It, too, is characterized by a contin-
uing rejection of and rebellion against God. The gospel does
not mean by this that the same historical conflict recurs or
is reenacted. The situation in this epoch of history is different from the one previous because the world of opposition has, to use legal terminology, "lost the case." Let us
use an analogy here. When a higher law court reaches a
verdict in a major case, its decision has a bearing on all
other related cases, even those in the lower courts. In a

similar way, the gospel declares the ultimate verdict which God has pronounced. The task of the church, consequently, is not to win people over to a particular view or way of life, but to present an ultimatum through its witness to and affirmation of the verdict made by God regarding human-kind, namely, that whoever believes in and confesses the authority of Jesus receives eternal life. Whoever does not believe is already condemned on the basis of the verdict spoken by God. Let us carry our analogy a bit further. Let us say that the lower courts have not yet acknowledged the verdict of the higher court, and therefore the case must be pleaded. Thus, in the period of the church, the legal process continues even though the actual outcome is already known. The final judgment day will come at the close of history, the purpose of which is to reinforce the end result of the process between God and the world, something al-ready quite clear from the death of Jesus.

The general historical view in the gospel is thought of in legal categories with Christ as the focal point. History is a cosmic process between God and the world, and in the end right shall inevitably prevail.

We must ask if the author of John is justified in his inter-pretation of Christ. Does he not present us with a radical reinterpretation of the historical Jesus?

We have already pointed out the distinct differences be-tween the synoptic Gospels and the Fourth Gospel regard-ing their presentation of the life and history of Jesus. We shall not go further into detail about this except to mention one very significant item. Jesus speaks very differently in John from the other three. He uses different words and different concepts. The theme which dominates Jesus' lan-guage in the other gospels is the kingdom of God, or, in other words God's supreme rule over the world. In the gospel of John, on the other hand, Jesus refers again and again to himself. If we ask ourselves, What about the bare, external facts?, then the gospel of John must give way to the other gospels. If we ask a similar question, What happened in Jesus' life at definite times and in definite places and what was actually said about him on various occasions?, then we would have to conclude that the gospel of John is less historical than the other gospels. If we attempt to make a critical reconstruction of Jesus' life, the other gospels are more "reliable" than the gospel of John. The description of Jesus' preaching in these gospels is far more varied, versatile, and differentiated. In the case of John we have a much simpler presentation, even a stylized rendering of Jesus' preaching. This does not imply, however, that the Fourth Gospel is without historical value, even in the modern sense of the term. There are several historical bits of information in this gospel which exhibit a high degree of historical reliability. We may mention elements of the passion story such as the Good Friday account (Jesus' day of death is one day earlier than in the other gospels, 18:28), the account concerning John the Baptist, 1:19ff.; 3:23ff., and further Jesus' three visits to Jerusalem, 5:1; 7:10; 12:12. But when it comes to reliable historicity, generally speaking, John must give way to the other gospels.

But we must not wrongly assume that, by reinterpreting history, the gospel makes Jesus into something he in reality was not and that, therefore, the gospel portrayal of Christ is not true. Perhaps we may even go so far as to say that the Fourth Gospel may in fact give us a truer picture of Jesus than do the other gospels.

This must be explained further. The author never saw his task as the reconstruction of a historical biography. This he neither would nor could do without at the same time twisting and falsifying the facts. His purpose is rather to point out the significance Jesus has for humankind, during

Jesus' own lifetime and at the time the gospel was being written. The author portrays Jesus deliberately and consciously from the viewpoint of faith. For him this is the only real Jesus. Any other Jesus than the Jesus of faith does not exist. Were one to attempt a life of Jesus apart from the perspective of faith, one would end up with an unintelligible fragment. It must be remembered that for the author and for the church as a whole, Jesus was not a remote person from the past, but the vanquisher of death, the exalted, living Lord. This Lord is not silent but continues to be heard, placing criteria before people by confronting them with decisions about God and their own lives. Jesus, then, is not only past but present. He has an everlasting significance, in that our history with God will always depend on the position we take with regard to him and his Word.

Is this to confuse history? If we inquire as to Jesus' own intentions and the understanding he had about his own role, as far as we can investigate these things, our answer will be a resolute "no." He has, on the basis of what we term the genuine words of Jesus, bound our eternal destiny and future inseparably to his own person (Mark 8:38). He did not, so far as we know, use messianic titles such as Messiah or Son of God to describe himself. (The one exception is that he may have used the term Son of man in relation to himself.) The fact that he did not is probably due to the fact that he is well aware that his contemporaries had given these terms inaccurate meanings. He wanted to be, not less, but more than what his Jewish contemporaries placed in these titles. He wanted to be something more than a Messiah as a politico-religious figure; he was rather to stand in God's stead over against humankind. The gospel of John clarifies this position in stressing statements which say that Jesus was with the Father, that he performs the Father's will, that he is one with the Father, etc.

Another question we could ask is why John does not mechanically repeat the words of Jesus as they one time must have been spoken. Why does he use other words, concepts, and forms than those which Jesus may have used himself? One factor may be the surroundings in which the gospel was written. Another, more plausible factor, may be that for the author of John simply repeating Jesus' words would be to bind and limit his significance. They are, after all, words arising out of the immediate situation; what is still more necessary is that eternally valid truths be given expression. For that matter, Jesus addressed himself *to* people rather than speaking *about* people. Jesus therefore has significance, not only for his own time and surroundings, but for people of all ages. In the gospel of John, Jesus uses both his own words and the words of the author to emphasize that his significance lies in the fact that he addresses people directly and that he is humanity's destiny even beyond his death. That his words have significance beyond his death does not mean that they bear spiritual force or that his words live on. If this were the case, it would be important for the author to record them literally. The gospel of John recognizes that Jesus speaks directly to people and thereby confronts them with God. This understanding is based on the resurrection, which in the gospel of John, gives Jesus' words everlasting validity. Jesus does not come to a person via his posthumous fame, but directly and by his own power. More consistently than any other gospel, the gospel of John presents the figure of Jesus as all-important for the destiny of humankind. In the evangelist's portrayal of Jesus also as a historical person, there is an inseparable bond between the account about Jesus and the confession of Jesus. This is the interpretation of history and the understanding of it on the basis of faith. To what extent this understanding of the person of Jesus is right or wrong cannot be determined scientifically. Only a personal decision can lead to such knowledge. But we cannot doubt that whatever language the author of this gospel uses, there is no discrepancy between this language and the intentions of Jesus.

FIVE

Life—from This Moment and through All Eternity

The Fourth Gospel, as indicated earlier, portrays Jesus as the one in whom the final revelation of God confronts humankind. Jesus therefore performs divine functions such as creating life and pronouncing judgment. We have already examined the unique thought that the act of judgment as well as the day or time of judgment are moved to within the arena of history. We shall now move on to another important motif in the gospel, namely, eternal life. Just as judgment becomes a phenomenon which takes place in time, eternal life, too, takes on a similar interpretation.

We shall first look at some religio-historical themes in order to place the understanding of the gospel into proper perspective.

It should already be familiar to us that the Old Testament does not have any specific understanding concerning a life after death other than a few peripheral references. There is no real belief in the resurrection and consequently no descriptions of an eternal life, that is to say, life understood as a timeless, unlimited existence after death. Passages which speak about eternal life or eternal time have quite another meaning; for example, an existence which in dimensions and quality extend beyond anything we know here. The whole matter of eternal life and the resurrection of the dead is not an Old Testament concern. The main emphasis is that God is eminently the God of this life. To possess life now is the supreme good gift. A long life, "to live long upon the land," is the mark of special favor and grace. Those who die young are looked upon as sinners. Death is the conclusion, the end, of all God-given life.

It is first in late Judaism that the notion of a resurrection begins to emerge, and then neither by chance nor as the result of direct borrowing from neighboring religions, as we are often given the impression through literature. The reason that the concept of the resurrection gained ground, though only very gradually, in the Jewish-Israelite religion, is due to the legal understanding of justice. God is emphasized more and more as the God of justice and a just God who seeks to establish justice in the world. Unfortunately, human experience tells one that justice has not yet been established in the world. History is not the record of its establishment.

If God is the God of justice, while history is the arena of injustice, the problem finds a solution in the belief in the resurrection. All righteousness and justice is fulfilled at the time of judgment. The injustices and inequities of this life can be made right after death. Belief in the resurrection gives birth to a belief in eternal life, which we know from late Judaism, and which we might express simply as life.

This life, a gift from God, is not only to be understood quantitatively, i.e., as endless time. It may certainly be understood also as this, because the sovereignty of death is broken. But eternal life is better understood qualitatively, that is, as a continuation of earthly existence, but without illness, want, unrighteousness, war, and above all, injustice. The most important element of eternal life, however, is an unbroken relationship with God, in which one is close to God and sees God. An additional point must also be made. The concept of eternal life is not understood first and foremost in an individual way; it is not just the resurrection of the individual that is of concern here. Quite the contrary, the concept of eternal life is bound together with the understanding of the end of history and the destiny of all humankind. The resurrection will take place in the last days, at the end of time, when we shall be raised up to eternal life in a new world. The eternal life, a life lived without interruption in nearness to God, will come at some future time. The kingdom of God and eternal life belong together.

This Jewish thinking reappears in primitive Christianity. The gospel of John, however, adds its own unique interpretation. This will become evident as we turn to several characteristic references: "Truly, truly, I say to you, he who hears my word and believes in him who sent me, has eternal life; he does not come into judgment, but has passed from death to life. Truly, truly, I say to you, the hour is coming, and now is, when the dead will hear the voice of the Son of God, and those who hear will live" (5:24-25). "Truly, truly, I say to you, he who believes has eternal life" (6:47). Perhaps this is the most specific of these passages: "And this is eternal life, that they know thee the only true God and Jesus Christ whom thou hast sent" (17:3). The same thought is also expressed in such texts as 3:16; 3:36; 6:40,54; and 11:26.

The emphasis of these texts is that what is most often regarded as a future event for determining the significance of humankind and the world and what will usher in a new world together with eternal life, is brought into the present. Future events are brought into the present when a person's life is brought before God and into a state of unimpeded fellowship with him. This is not to say, however, that either the gospel of John or any other New Testament writings espouse the immortality of the soul. Neither life nor death are to be understood as natural phenomena. Life is the gift of the Creator, and he can take it back again. Therefore, eternal life is not something a person has because of an immortal soul; one may have it if God, of his own free will, chooses to give it. The Creator's absolute independence is necessary for a true understanding of humankind. We are mortal; death is our fate and lot so long as we are left to ourselves. This is one of the primary emphases in the presentation of Christ in the gospel of John. Since God speaks through the words of Jesus, Jesus is the only one who "has life in himself"; i.e., he possesses the divine creative power which gives life (1:4; 5:21,26; 6:35,48; 10:10,28; 17:2).

This thought is most lucidly formulated in 11:25: "I am the resurrection and the life." It is also clear in 14:6 where Jesus declares, "I am the way, and the truth, and the life." In other words, Christ not only speaks about eternal life, he not only promises eternal life, he not only mediates eternal life—he *is* eternal life. Life does not exist apart from him. Life is one of the attributes of God, and we are brought face to face with it when confronted with Jesus. Eternal life as understood by the evangelist's Jewish contemporaries signified the perfect revelation of God himself and thus a new mode of existence. The evangelist tells his readers that the full and complete revelation of the Father and of the future kingdom in which he reigns supreme has now been given. This revelation will not come at some future point, but is ushered into the here and now. Hence, the transition from death to life occurs right now by means of faith.

Thus, John transfers the focal point of a life from the moment of death, as well as the end of the world, to a moment in the present. This new focal point is the encounter with God's Son who is the basis for the new existence. It is also clear that the Fourth Gospel uses the concepts "life" and "death" in something other than a purely biological/physical sense. To possess life means to be dependent upon God and to have fellowship with him in truth; death, on the other hand, is to be in a state of falsehood before God and to have illusions about the nature of humankind. The one type of existence has already been condemned to irrevocable defeat, while nothing can ever touch or affect the other. The gospel certainly admits the reality of physical death, but this no longer marks something decisive. The outcome of physical death is already known by the manner in which a person responds to ultimate reality, i.e., to God himself as he reveals himself in Jesus. The gospel of John states this with unmistakable clarity in the words of Jesus: "I am the resurrection and the life; he who believes in me, though he die, yet shall he live, and whoever lives and believes in me shall never die" (11:25-26). Physical death is conquered in the sense that the turning point it normally designates in one's existence is anticipated and "experienced" in the confrontation with the revelation of God: "Truly, truly, I say to you, he who hears my word and believes him who sent me, has eternal life; he does not come into judgment, but has passed from death to life" (5:24). The new mode of existence is eternal in the sense that it is not subject to death or any judgmental action on the part of God. Since eternal life—this genuinely new form of life—is exclusively related to Christ, it follows that access to it is only to be had through faith in him (3:15-16; 5:24; 6:40,47). Faith is not the same thing as assuming there is eternal life, but belief in Jesus Christ. This means taking a definite position with regard to him, trusting that he represents the Father, divine reality, so that through him and by him one receives this new existence or real life as a gift.

For the time being, we shall not say anything further about the nature of faith. Instead, we shall consider the characteristics of the new life, about which the gospel is clear. We shall first refer to a text in 1 John. Although the epistle did not have the same author as the gospel, it stemmed from the same Christian community, but from a later generation. The text to which we now turn summarizes well a number of statements made in the gospel: "We know that we have passed out of death into life, because we love the brethren. He who does not love abides in death. Any one who hates his brother is a murderer, and you know that no murderer has eternal life abiding in him. By this we know love, that he laid down his life for us; and we ought to lay down our lives for the brethren. But if any one has the world's goods and sees his brother in need, yet closes his heart against him, how does God's love abide in him?" (1 John 3:14ff.).

Thus, the new mode of existence, referred to as eternal life, consists of love, *agape* in Greek. This is intimately related to the understanding of God's own nature, which is precisely characterized as love or *agape:* "He who does not love does not know God; for God is love" (1 John 4:8). The Father and the Son have life which creates. This life is love and is the key to knowing why we were brought into existence, a secret brought into the open by Jesus. In revealing this fact, he has also manifested the real life. As God's representative, Jesus reveals the aspects of this life in such a lowly task as washing the disciples' feet. Love becomes a sacrament in that the foot washing takes place in the gospel of John at the point where the other gospels record the institution of the Lord's Supper. Eternal life,

understood as love, receives its most specific and most paradoxical manifestation in the death of Jesus: "He laid down
his life for us" (1 John 3:16); paradoxical because life here
finds its expression in one's self-denial of life for the sake
of others. The distinguishing features of this love are not
primarily emotional, but rooted in an attitude which man-
ifests itself in actions. The two go hand in hand. This life
as love, however, is exclusively related to Jesus. One does
not possess it automatically, but only in constant fellowship
with Jesus. It is thus given constantly to people. This notion
is clearly stated in the metaphor of the vine and the branches (15:9ff.). Eternal life—unbroken fellowship with the Father—reveals itself not in a mystical, inner experience, but
through actual, specific deeds as the outgrowth of love. It
is in this love relationship that one really begins to com-
prehend something of the nature of God (13:35). If we now
make a connection between this and the introduction, we
see that the concept of Jesus as the Son of God, and the
revelation of God, comes to light as he gives us the ability
and the courage to love, *agape*. *Agape* shows us who God
is. There is therefore only one commandment: "This is my
commandment, that you love one another as I have loved
you. Greater love has no man than this, that a man lay
down his life for his friends" (15:12-13). This is characterized
as the commandment of eternal life. It is in this connection
the concept "truth" becomes clear to us, a major term in
this gospel. For the author of John, truth, in the Christian
sense, is a person (14:6). This is an expression of the divine
truth. Love as the expression of God's nature and truth
fuses all together into a single entity. We are thus not placed
up against two separate aspects of existence, i.e., love as
effect and truth as theoretical knowledge. The two become
one in that they, though somewhat differently, both express
the same divine truth by which one truly becomes oneself,

namely, in the proper understanding of what it is to be human.

There is one more statement concerning eternal life which we must consider, a passage very often referred to and quoted: "And this is eternal life, that they know thee the only true God, and Jesus Christ whom thou hast sent" (17:3). Eternal life is understood here as a specific form of confession, namely knowing and acknowledging God. We must consider what this implies in the gospel of John.

To do this, we must be aware of the fact that there is a difference between the Greek and Hebrew concepts of knowledge and knowing. Hebrew thought, for our purposes, is the more important, since it provides the background for the gospel of John. To know or to have knowledge in the Old Testament implies much more than simply being an observer; it is more than the accumulation of facts by which the seeker of knowledge determines what implications a person or thing has for himself. Knowledge is more than what we today might call an objective recording of data and the analysis of phenomena. To know, in the Old Testament, means primarily that one has experience with something in a direct and subjective sense. One may speak about knowing only after one has had first-hand experience of and emotional involvement with whatever it is that affects one's own existence. The object is not itself essential, but its effect on and significance for our lives are all-important. Old Testament thought can be understood only when personal relationships and involvement are taken into consideration. To know, then, is much more than a mere thought process: emotion, intellect, and will are all involved.

This becomes a bit more clear when we distinguish between "to understand" and "to know about something," i.e., to make use of insight and knowledge. To know God is not only to have knowledge about him and his nature, but to acknowledge his significance, will, and requirements for a person. Therefore, one can only have knowledge which materializes itself in action, in practice. To know is to allow one's life and deeds to be determined by what one knows. God is known by a person only when that person permits himself or herself to be motivated and directed by what God demands, does, and wills.

This being said, let us return to the final statement concerning eternal life in the gospel of John (17:3, see also above) which says that eternal life consists in knowing the only true God and Jesus Christ whom he has sent. This does not mean that we are to have a certain amount of objective knowledge about God, but rather that we let our life and existence be characterized, determined, and dominated by God. God himself is life, eternal life, in the sense explained above. To know him is therefore to allow oneself to be influenced by God's own nature. It is as one participates in the very life of God that one *has* eternal life. But this life, as we have seen, cannot be understood apart from "the one sent out." To know God is thus possible only because God, of his own free will, seeks fellowship with us. To make God the object of logical, analytical speculation and study is to place him outside the realm of our being able to know him.

We must also point out that according to Old Testament and late Jewish thought the possibility of really knowing God belonged to the future beyond the grave. For the gospel of John, however, this possibility exists within the realm of history through an historic person. This gospel maintains that all knowledge of God is dependent upon one's relationship to this person. This knowledge signifies the only valid, genuine state of being, the criterion of which is love.

We look once again to 1 John: "Beloved, let us love one another; for love is of God, and he who loves is born of God and knows God. He who does not love does not know God; for God is love" (1 John 4:7-8). It is clearly understood throughout the gospel of John that knowledge of God comes about through Jesus, the Son. Direct knowledge of God is therefore excluded because God is not accessible to us except through his revelation in Jesus. The gospel also declares that it is in knowing Jesus as the Son of God and being in a personal relationship to him that one is able to know God.

SIX

Via Dolorosa— God's Own Way

The passion story is the climax of the Fourth Gospel. In it we find expressed most paradoxically that Jesus, as the Son of God, is the "bearer" of divine truth, since the fact that he is the Son of God becomes evident primarily in his suffering and death. Early Christianity had to grapple with the problem of a Messiah who suffered and died and thereby endured defeat. This posed a difficult problem for the transmission of the tradition; here was an enigmatic, puzzling event, for which an explanation was necessary. For the Fourth Gospel, however, the passion and death of Jesus pose no problem whatsoever.

Generally speaking, the presentation of the passion story in the gospel of John portrays the same events as the other gospels. The basic outline includes many of the same events: Jesus' arrest, his trials before the Jewish and Roman authorities, pronouncement of the death sentence, the crucifixion, death, and burial. But we discover some rather striking differences in comparing John's account with that of Mark, and not merely in the many inconsistencies concerning historical details. The real difference is rather one of theological perspective and interpretation of the events. This is particularly discernible in the manner in which Mark describes the person and suffering of Jesus. Mark gives us a clear, detailed picture of deep derision and humiliation. At the close of his life, Jesus is despised and rejected by all. His suffering is greatly intensified by his being totally isolated. He is rejected not only by his own people, but Mark emphasizes that he is rejected even by his disciples. He is delivered into the hands of those who do with him as they wish. Even God forsakes him in the final moments of his life, as is so dramatically indicated by his desolate cry, "My God, my God, why hast thou forsaken me?" (Mark 15:34).

John describes the situation differently. There are many similarities, of course, both with regard to the main events and the absence of any description of torture. The same is true of the attempt to describe the suffering psychologically. Further, the death scene itself is barely mentioned. All the gospels report the events of the passion with a calmness that is almost amazing. The difference—in this instance between Mark and John—reveals itself most clearly in the portrayal of Jesus. This is best seen as we first note some characteristics from Mark which are lacking in John. The first is the Gethsemane scene (Mark 14:26-42) describing Jesus' struggle with himself concerning the events before him. A second significant difference, which involves not merely something omitted but rather a direct contradiction of Mark by John, is that Mark tells us that a certain man from Cyrene helped carry the cross of Christ. John, on the other hand, emphasizes that Jesus carried it alone (19:17). In the third place, John says nothing about the signs which occurred following the death of Jesus—the signs which were

manifestations of the divine in the midst of tragic circumstances, such as the eclipse, earthquake, the tearing of the
temple curtain from top to bottom, the dead arising from
their graves, etc. (Mark 15:38; Matthew 27:51-54). In John
the spotlight is always on the person of Jesus; all peripheral
events fade into the background. Fourthly, John says nothing of the mockery Jesus endured while on the cross (Mark
15:29-32). Finally, John does not record Jesus' cry before
dying (Mark 15:37).

It is in making these comparisons between the passion
story in John and the other gospels that we begin to understand the aims of the Fourth Gospel. The most striking
contrast is that in the Fourth Gospel there is no mention
of Jesus being delivered into the hands of men who can do
with him as they please. It is emphasized time and again
that Jesus himself willed his death and determined when
it would take place. The arrest scene is typical: those who
sought to arrest Jesus could not arrest him without his willingness to cooperate. His would-be captors could only fall
to the ground in his presence. Since they shrank from per-
forming their task, Jesus, in a very real sense, had to bring
about his own arrest (18:1-11). He sharply rebukes Peter
for his attempt to rescue him (18:10-11). In the trial scenes
before the Jewish leaders (18:19ff.) and Pilate (18:33ff.) Jesus
does not remain largely silent as in the gospel of Mark but
takes the initiative. By directing the conversation and forc-
ing Pilate to his question of resignation, "What is truth?",
Jesus indicates that Pilate has absolutely no power over him
(19:11). The death scene (19:23-28) shows that Jesus was
able to determine the time of his death, which he permitted
to happen only when he was certain his life's work had been
accomplished (19:30).

Through the entire account we are given a picture, not
of one who is handed over, nor of one who is the object of

persecution, but of one who himself acts and determines the events in the midst of suffering and persecution. One might be tempted to go so far as to characterize Jesus' death as suicidal. At any rate, the purpose of the entire account is to reveal that what takes place is in accordance with the will and plan of Jesus. This assertion can be made not only on the basis of the events, but by several challenging and provocative statements as well, for example: "For this reason the Father loves me, because I lay down my life, that I may take it again. No one takes it from me, but I lay it down of my own accord. I have power to lay it down, and I have power to take it again; this charge I have received from my Father" (10:17-18). Jesus is in full control of the events and of himself. No one in this world can force him to do anything he does not himself wish to do. According to the gospel of John, Jesus is not directed to the cross by meaningless, adverse fate, nor is it death by outward hostility which strikes him down. He willingly goes to the cross, in perfect obedience, as one who is sent there by God. He goes to his death in God's stead, in absolute dedication to the will of God. The fulfillment of God's will was his goal. With this, the gospel of John emphasizes several definite things.

Jesus' last words, "It is finished" (19:30), clearly indicate that his death cannot be understood as a hostile plot by his enemies to terminate his life's work or to cut it off so that his work must be resumed following the resurrection. Quite the contrary, Jesus' suffering and death take place as an integral part of his mission; in fact, they are the climax of what he came to do. The gospel uses some expressions which may sound strange to us, but which emphasize the significance of Jesus' death. First, the death on the cross is called a means of "glorification" because it reveals the divine glory, i.e., the glory and radiance of God (see 12:16,23; 13:32; 17:1,5). The Fourth Gospel maintains that the divine makes a breakthrough in Jesus' death on the cross. God is revealed not primarily in the resurrection or the ascension, but in the death of Jesus. Second, the gospel of John uses the expression to "lift up" (3:14; 8:28; 12:32,34). We have previously indicated that the evangelist is fond of using terms which may have a double meaning. The Greek term to "lift up" can mean to lift up or hang up (as on the cross), or to elevate, to make high in the sense of bestowing honor, to exalt, to be lifted up to God. The gospel of John characteristically combines these, for it understands that in being lifted up on the cross, Jesus is being exalted. His being lifted up is an occasion of honor. It is thus not the ascension which is the ultimate sign of exaltation, but rather being lifted up upon the tree of execution. Herein lies the Johannine paradox, namely, in the clash between the visible, apparently catastrophic events and humiliation, and that these are understood as the climax of divine glory revealing God's own innermost being.

There are a number of statements in the gospel which explain how its author understood this. We shall refer to only a few.

Jesus says, "I am the good shepherd. The good shepherd lays down his life for the sheep" (10:11). "Shepherd" is not only a descriptive illustration, but a term familiar from the Old Testament and rabbinic literature used to refer to God himself. Another applicable statement: "Greater love has no man than this, that a man lay down his life for his friends" (15:13). Also: "And for their sake (i.e., the disciples) I consecrate myself . . . " (17:19). He devotes himself and offers himself for his disciples. There is also this paradoxical statement: "He who loves his life loses it, and he who hates his life in this world will keep it for eternal life" (12:25).

The key word in all these statements, as well as the passion story, is love, *agape*. This word forms a thread of continuity throughout. Jesus reveals the very nature of God, which is love. It reaches its zenith in dedication and sacrifice for others. This self-sacrificial aspect of love is emphasized in the death of Jesus, which is the supreme expression of the nature of God. The entire passion story could be summed up in Jesus' words: "For God so loved the world that he gave his only Son, that whoever believes in him should not perish but have eternal life" (3:16). Nowhere is the nature of God—who and what he is—more clearly defined than here. For the gospel of John it is not primarily miracles which reveal the power of God, although the evangelist is not unfamiliar with the miraculous. It is not such signs as earthquakes, the dead rising up out of their graves, or the appearance of angels which reveal God to us, but simply the act of love carried out in the death of Jesus. As we have already indicated, his death is the means by which he is glorified.

The word *glory* in the Scriptures is a technical term used to denote the nature of God. More specifically, it stands for the radiancy which surrounds God's person. In the gospel of John, the glory of God is understood primarily as the love of God. Thus, 1:14 states another paradox in describing the "human" Jesus: "We have beheld his glory, glory as of the only Son of the Father." Jesus had no outward characteristics which distinguished him from anyone else; certainly he bore no conspicuous, external signs of divine glory. This is precisely the point, for he is not known by his appearance, but by his supreme sacrifice which reveals the love of God. As the gospel portrays the conflict between Jesus and the Jews, the accusation is repeatedly made against Jesus that he, a mere man, makes himself equal to God (5:18; 10:33; 19:7). His enemies could not attach any divine attributes to him on the basis of his appearance. They thus consider his claims false and blasphemous. But at the same time, the gospel discloses that they who fail to recognize God in the person of Jesus do not in reality know God and cannot understand anything about him. Had they known him, i.e., had they understood that God's nature is revealed in all-encompassing, self-giving love, they would have realized that Jesus represents him, and that the cross was necessarily a climax of the revelation of God. Had the disciples understood this, they would not have objected to the footwashing (13:1ff.) but would have realized that just such a humiliating and unselfish act explains who God is (13:1,34). The footwashing scene foreshadows his impending death. Viewed apart from faith, Jesus' passion and death are, of course, signs of humiliation, disgrace, and shame, but seen with the eyes of faith, these events attest to the love and glory of God.

From this it should be clear why it was so essential that Jesus should be portrayed as willingly choosing death rather than being forced to die against his will. This shows that it was God who was acting in and through Jesus. God, who is free and sovereign, is not coerced to anything by anyone. As the supreme act of love, Jesus' death had to be a voluntary death, and it had to take place for the sake of others. Again the arrest scene shows that the event does not occur for Jesus' own sake. Jesus brings about his own arrest, for example, on the condition that his disciples be allowed to go free (18:8-9). This indicates that he gives his life for the sake of others.

Death, as we have seen, is the means by which Jesus is glorified, or to state it a bit differently, it is the means by which Jesus returned to the Father. We have seen that, as the Son of God, Jesus reveals that the all-powerful God who holds humankind in the palm of his hand is also a merciful

Father, one who loves. He is the reason for our having existence. In the moment Jesus offers his life as an act of love, he declares his faith in this loving Father. He does not, therefore, deliver himself into the hands of death, but gives himself to the Author of life. He returns in love to the One who is love. The resurrection affirms the fact that Jesus, in death, has not entered into nothingness or oblivion, but by his sacrifice has gone to the Father. The resurrection is the pronouncement of God's verdict: Apparent failure has become victory because it perfectly demonstrates God's innermost being. On the other hand, apparent victory has turned into failure, for in the rejection of Jesus' love, God too has been rejected. The bitter irony of this is shown in these words: "They cried out, 'Away with him, away with him, crucify him!' Pilate said to them, 'Shall I crucify your King?' The chief priests answered, 'We have no king but Caesar.' " (19:15). The terrible irony here is that the emperor, Caesar, usurps God's rightful place, and it is the chosen people of God, with all their faith in him, who reject the Son of God and choose the emperor instead.

It is in paradox and irony that God's nature as love and the nature of eternal life is revealed. The climax of God's love is revealed in the sacrifice of the Son. No greater love has any man than that he lay down his life. It is only in this event that knowledge and understanding of God are brought to completeness and perfection. Therefore, the final words of Jesus are: "It is finished" (19:30). He dies knowing that his work is accomplished and brought to completion. But in this supreme act of love he becomes one with the Father; he is in fellowship with him forever, i.e., he now lives eternally.

SEVEN

Nothing Separates
Jesus and the Believer

The story of Jesus does not conclude with his suffering
and death, nor with his return to the Father. What is said
about his offering up of himself and his exaltation is the key
to understanding the life and nature of the church as presented in the Fourth Gospel. It is in this regard that the
uniqueness of the gospel of John becomes apparent. This
gospel does not use the word *church* or any of the terms
commonly used for the church in the remainder of the New
Testament. One of the unresolved questions among scholars
is why the gospel of John does not record the institution of
the Lord's Supper; the author is familiar with Holy Com-
munion but says nothing about its origin. The Fourth Gospel has no institutional concept of the church, i.e., as an
impersonal structure. The church is not presented as an
organization, nor is any space given to its growth and development. No ecclesiastical offices or ordinances are listed;
church leaders and clergy simply are not mentioned. Not
even the word *apostle* appears in its usual sense; it is used
only once, and then in another way than is ordinary for the
rest of the New Testament.

All of this can be explained. That the gospel of John excludes from its account any notion of institution and organization is to signify how strictly personal is its understanding of the church, and the gospel clearly chooses to omit the word *church*. We could in a slogan-like manner characterize the understanding of the gospel in this way: The church is no organization but an organism. Typical also at this point in the account is the same strong concentration on Jesus, otherwise familiar to us in the gospel. Christ is the center of the organism which is comprised of those who are believers. The church, for the Fourth Gospel, is a manifestation of the person of Christ. This has several aspects.

It was commonly understood among early Christians that, following his death and resurrection, Christ would at some time return in all his divine majesty and glory. This would mark the conclusion of human history and the end of time. The writer of the gospel of John was familiar with the expectation of the return of Christ, but he also gives this a unique interpretation. The theme of Jesus' return appears repeatedly in the so-called farewell discourse (Chapters 14–18), and is understood in this way: The second coming of Christ occurs immediately following his resurrection. He comes through his Holy Spirit and Word to all who believe in him (14:18ff.; 16:16ff.). The church, then, is primarily the manifestation of the presence of Christ among believers. The Spirit is indicative of his presence among people. It is a mistake to suppose that when Christ returned to the Father his place had to be filled here by a substitute, be it Spirit, doctrines, ecclesiastics, or whatever. There is no distance to be overcome between the historical Jesus and the Christ of the church. There is no distance between heaven and earth, for Jesus Christ continues to be present here on earth and is actively at work among those who are his. This is most vividly expressed in the metaphor of Chapter 15, which speaks of the vine and the branches. Jesus is the vine, those who believe in him are the branches. They are joined, and thus believers are in continual and direct contact with him. This deeply personal relationship must not be overshadowed by any concept of institutions, organizational structures, or hierarchies. Jesus says: "He who abides in me and I in him, he it is that bears much fruit, for apart from me you can do nothing" (15:5). Apart from Jesus, there can be no relationship with God. The manner in which the presence of Christ is made specific is a matter to which we shall return shortly.

It cannot be emphasized too strongly that for the gospel writer the church is (1) Christ, and (2) his people. Once again, the gospel guards against every impersonal representation of the assembly of the faithful. It is those who believe in Christ who constitute the church. The church is thus the sum of a definite group of people. The question is, which group of people? The answer to this question must also come from the significance of Jesus' death, which, as we have seen in the Fourth Gospel, is a trial between God and the world, in which judgment is passed upon humankind. Or, to state it differently, we bring judgment upon ourselves by virtue of the position we take with regard to the person of Jesus. For whatever position we take brings about divisions among people—between those on the one hand who acknowledge the divine authority of Jesus, and those on the other who deny it. We should keep in mind that for the author of John, the church already existed at the time of the events which he records; namely, the time of Israel, the Jewish people, who were both a nation and a church. The people of Israel were confronted with a choice concerning the revelation of Jesus which culminated in his death. Their decision revealed his death for what it was and them for what they were. They believed that in passing judgment upon Jesus and condemning him to death, he received the punishment which his blasphemy so justly deserved. The great tragedy is that they, the "people of God," used their religious heritage and traditions, even their faith and their Scriptures, as the basis for their denial of Jesus as the One who reveals the Father. They believed that the law, their freedom, and even God were their rightful possessions; they wanted no new and disruptive revelation of God as love. They refused to accept and believe that their life and existence is always a gift from the Creator. Thus, they lied about their own existence.

The church is therefore the assembly and the total of all those who acknowledge that the death of Jesus is the supreme revelation of the nature and will of God. They thereby arrive at a new and genuine understanding of their life as a gift, and life means a continual dependence upon God himself. A proper understanding of Jesus gives us a proper understanding of ourselves. The church, then, may simply be characterized as consisting of those "who are of the truth," i.e., those who believe that God speaks through Jesus and the events relating to him (10:3; 18:37).

This relationship to the significance of Jesus' death is, however, not an impersonal relationship or an idea or a thought. The gospel stresses the necessity for a personal relationship to God as Father. Hence, the strong emphasis upon faith which brings one into a direct, personal relationship with the Father. To be of the truth means to live in relationship with and in dependence on God for whom the Son is mediator. The church can therefore not be understood apart from its relationship to the Son. The church is much more than an institution based upon adherence to doctrines, as is shown by the importance placed upon one's relationship to Jesus.

How thorough the author of the gospel is reveals itself here. We have repeatedly said that the nature of God is revealed through Jesus as love and as fellowship. The church is to reflect this love of God in its own life. It is underscored repeatedly that this love is the sure sign of the church's presence. Those who constitute the church must stand united in dedication, fellowship, and love. That Jesus always gave of himself, even in death, establishes the conditions of the church's life and existence. Although there are several texts to which we could refer, we shall turn to only one which summarizes them all. It is the account of the footwashing, to which we have earlier made reference. It contains two important and distinct elements. The first section (13:1-11), states the basic condition for the church exemplified in the humble act of Jesus who shows his love for others in serving them. He offers not only his love, but himself. The second section (13:12-17), contains Jesus' command to his disciples that they wash each other's feet, i.e., that they serve each other. Loving service is shown to be the valid confession of Jesus as the revealer of God's love, i.e., God's real nature. These same elements appear in the discourse about the vine and the branches (with sections corresponding to the above text, 15:1-10 and 11-15. See also 13:34). Here it is emphasized twice that the church has only one mandate, the commandment to love (15:12-17).

Closely related to this is the emphasis on the church being recognizable by its unity (17:20ff.). It is not organizational unity which is being referred to here, but a free and personal fellowship. This unity is to reflect the unity Jesus reveals as existing between the Father and the Son. The church is the church only when its members dwell together in unity and love, the sign that Jesus is personally in their midst.

The concept of the church is so centered around the person of Christ, and his personal closeness gives it such an inner dynamic, that it would be impossible for the church to become a static institution without it actually ceasing to be the church. One is not granted security either by the church as institution or by a system of doctrines. Security does not come from membership in the church. The gospel knows that it has drawn a picture of the true church, but its everyday life does not always meet the ideal standards set for it. Judas appears in the gospel as a representative of some who belong to the church, but who do not live the truth and therefore cease to remain in fellowship with Christ (6:64-65,70-71; 8:31; 13:6). Faith, therefore, is not something automatically present, but must continually be acquired. Believers must renew their faith (2:11; 11:15; 13:19; 14:29; 15:6). The members of the church are always being tested. It has been said that the author of the gospel of Mark hates the Twelve, i.e., the inner circle of the disciples. This is a provocative way of stating that Mark hurls sharp criticism against the church. Nor is the gospel of John without criticism of the church. The true church is made up of all those, both within and without the church framework, who live in absolute obedience to Christ and reflect him in their lives. It is they who are of the truth.

As a manifestation of the life of God, the church cannot live unto itself. Some scholars have been perplexed at the lack of a developed theology of mission in the Fourth Gospel. But the task of the church is definitely underscored in several places, such as 17:18ff.; and 20:31. Just as Jesus was sent into the world by the Father, so too the church is sent by Jesus to the world. The relationship which exists between Jesus and the Father is reflected in the relationship which exists between Jesus and the church. Jesus sends the church out to reach people; its task is to give the world the possibility of faith (17:21). We note here that the church is not sent to the individual, nor is its being sent out just one of several tasks. The church's entire reason for existing is to approach the world so that it be given the possibility of coming to faith. There is no mission mandate as such, nor a specifically stated order, but this is due to the fact that the life of Jesus gives people the possibility of knowing God and having fellowship with him. Everything hinges upon this. The life of the church is understood as the continuation of Jesus' mission. Therefore the function of the church must be understood as that of giving people the opportunity to acknowledge Jesus as the one sent by God. If the church is anything other than this, it is no longer the church. It can fulfill and accomplish its task in only one way, and that is in the giving of its life whereby the nature of God may be known as revealed in the love of Christ. The entire life of the church must point to him.

EIGHT

The Counselor—
Jesus' Successor

In the synoptic Gospels, Jesus speaks about the kingdom of God; in the Fourth Gospel, he speaks about himself. We are justified in asserting that Jesus himself is the theme of the gospel of John. But this must be said with qualification, for it is in directing his attention exclusively to Jesus that the author attempts to bring the reader to a clear understanding of the nature and personhood of God. Jesus is the theme of the gospel because God reveals himself audibly and visibly through him. This is evident from the prologue to the gospel, which states the theme: "In the beginning was the Word, and the Word was with God, and the Word was God" (1:1).

The gospel of John also speaks about the Holy Spirit. In doing so, the Fourth Gospel speaks about God. The Spirit not only tells us what God does, but who he is. The outpouring of the Spirit is also an experiencing of God himself. This is evident from a statement unique for John: "God is spirit . . . " (4:24).

Early Christianity was characterized by the occurrence of what we today term charismatic phenomena. The word

charisma denotes heaven-sent, miraculous gifts of the Holy
Spirit. These gifts were channeled through persons who
radiated the divine in specific phenomena. The congregations witnessed sights and sounds; for example, healings,
signs, speaking in tongues, and prophets arise. The worship
services were marked by jubilant ecstasy. Primitive Christianity was anything but an intellectual movement. Charismatic signs were believed to be definite manifestations of
the Spirit and were common throughout virtually all early
Christian congregations. There was a simple factor behind
such widespread acceptance of these signs and why so much
importance was attached to them: It was believed that the
resurrected Jesus appeared to the world through these signs
which the Spirit used to break down barriers between persons and to bring them the liberating power of God. The
resurrected Christ used these ecstatic, miraculous phenomena to make himself known both to the world and to the
church. To have experienced the Holy Spirit in one's life
was also to have experienced the presence of the risen one.
These various charismatic phenomena were ongoing
expressions of his resurrection life. Jesus and the Holy Spirit
cannot therefore be separated.

The Holy Spirit is, as in the other gospels, important in
the Fourth Gospel. The evangelist speaks about God when
he speaks about the Spirit. The passage we cited above is
only a part of a text which directs itself to Christian worship
in the early church: "But the hour is coming, and now is,
when the true worshipers will worship the Father in spirit
and truth, for such the Father seeks to worship him. God
is spirit, and those who worship him must worship in spirit
and truth" (4:23-24).

These words reflect the oldest language and tradition
held in common by Christians regarding the Spirit, that is
to say, the inspired, charismatic worship service to which

we find references throughout the New Testament. We see here that the gospel of John has this in common with early Christianity. On the other hand, there appears to be little interest in the Fourth Gospel for the ecstatic and the emotional.

An element of worship called *glossolalia* or the speaking in tongues was common in early Christian congregations. In the Lukan and Pauline writings it is understood as the language of heaven which makes itself heard in the congregation. We search in vain in the Johannine writings for any account of speaking in tongues or other charismatic phenomena. The worship service here is also worship in the Spirit, but this is so because the service is understood as having a single purpose, a purpose or function like that which Christ has, namely, to reflect the nature of God. The worship service in the gospel of John is a service in the Spirit, not because charismatic events occur, but because God speaks in and through the service. Here again the Fourth Gospel shows its unique character. The gospel seeks only to get to the heart of the matter, i.e., to God himself. This is also true whenever the Spirit is discussed, because the Spirit represents the risen Jesus to the congregation. The evangelist stresses this as being the main factor behind the charismatic phenomena. He is not so interested in the phenomena themselves, but in what they mean. The phenomena point to the Spirit, the Spirit points to Jesus, and Jesus to God.

The Spirit, therefore, as elsewhere in the New Testament, cannot be understood apart from Jesus' resurrection: "He who believes in me, as the scripture has said, 'Out of his heart shall flow rivers of living water.' Now this he said about the Spirit, which those who believed in him were to receive; for as yet the Spirit had not been given, because Jesus was not yet glorified" (7:38-39). The glorification is a way of saying that Jesus is taken anew into the divine realm, that he is thus raised up from the dead. The close connection between the Spirit and the resurrection of Jesus is most clearly seen in the Johannine discourse about the Counselor, who is given following the death and resurrection of Jesus (Chapters 14–17).

Before going further, we must again bring to mind a matter we have already discussed. It is the importance of the words of Jesus in the Fourth Gospel. The Johannine church must be especially characterized as "the church of the Word" because in this gospel it is the assembly of those who hear the words of Jesus and, as the result of hearing, come to faith in him and God. In Jesus' testament or so-called farewell discourse (Chapters 14–17), the words by which the church shall live following Jesus' resurrection are those words which Jesus has spoken once and for all. It is constantly stressed that Jesus is the Lord of the church. But he remains Lord only so long as his words are determinative and binding for the believer (13:19; 14:23-24,29; 15:3,7,11; 16:1,4). We have the recorded word of Jesus in the gospels which enables us to do something which the author of the Fourth Gospel was unable to do, and that is to make a distinction between Jesus and his word in the same way that we are able to distinguish between a person and what that person says. For John, the connection between a person and his words is much closer than it would be for us. It was not possible for the writer that Jesus could exist apart from his words. Jesus is there where his word is; he and his words are one, a point made again and again. We shall only cite one text in this connection: "If a man loves me, he will keep my word, and my Father will love him, and we will come to him and make our home with him. He who does not love me does not keep my words; and the word which you hear is not mine but the Father's who sent me" (14:23-24). The point made here is clear enough: Jesus is there where his word is. But we must take this a step further and say that where Jesus' word is, there God is. Further, the text says that the word of Jesus is the word of God. This takes up once again the theme we have now heard so often, that God himself speaks and makes himself known through the words of Jesus. The reference, of course, is to the spoken, proclaimed word.

This brings us to a central point concerning what the Fourth Gospel says about the Spirit, for Jesus describes his words as spirit or the Spirit. "It is the spirit that gives life, the flesh is of no avail; the words that I have spoken to you are spirit and life" (6:63). "For he whom God has sent utters the words of God, for it is not by measure that he gives the Spirit" (3:34). These statements show us the intimate connection between the Spirit and the words of Jesus. There emerges a kind of "trinitarian" formula out of all this. In the first place, God is referred to as spirit; in the second place, the words of Jesus are regarded as being part of Jesus himself; in the third place, Jesus' words are said to be spirit.

This brings us to a decisive factor in the discussion of the Fourth Gospel regarding the Spirit. We discover here a unique term for the Holy Spirit not found outside the Johannine literature. The Spirit is called the Counselor or the Paraclete. In fact, the term can be used interchangeably with Holy Spirit, although the term appears only in the central section of the gospel, the testament or so-called farewell discourse (Chapters 14–17). This testament or discourse speaks about life following the death of Jesus, with emphasis upon the relationship between Jesus and the disciples. It is further discussed how Jesus' word in the future, i.e., after his death, shall be addressed to the world. The foundation for the church is the word of Jesus—those words which Jesus has spoken and have now been recorded in the gospel. Through his work, and now in the words of the farewell discourse, Jesus has provided the church with words by which it shall live. They shall guide the disciples, and they shall give guidance to the church and shall protect and preserve its life in the future (13:19; 14:29-30; 15:1; 16:1,4). We are, however, not to understand by this that Jesus lives on through his words. The life of the church is not to be understood in such a way that Jesus is present through the mere repetition of his words. It is here the Counselor or Paraclete comes into the picture. The Counselor has only one task according to the gospel of John, and that is to make known the words of Jesus and see to it that they are heard and obeyed: "But the Counselor, the Holy Spirit, whom the Father will send in my name, he will teach you all things, and bring to your remembrance all that I have said to you" (14:26). We should note that the Spirit brings definite words to remembrance, not the language in tongues. The church is therefore really the church of the Holy Spirit, a truly charismatic church, when Jesus' word is proclaimed, heeded, and obeyed.

The Greek word *paraklētos*, which we have translated "Counselor," could perhaps just as well have been translated "Preacher," for this is the essential task of the Spirit in the gospel of John. It is because of this task that John uses the term "remembrance": The Counselor will "bring to your remembrance all that I have said to you" (14:26, see above). This remembrance implies something more than seeing to it that certain things are remembered, or that they remain alive in one's memory; namely, that Jesus' words be remembered in such a way that they become binding for individuals and normative for the congregation. They are words to be obeyed. It is in this way that Jesus is and remains Lord of the church through his words. The gospel tends to be one-sided in its emphasis on the words of Jesus as expressing the Holy Spirit. "When the Spirit of truth comes, he will guide you into all the truth; for he will not speak on his own authority, but whatever he hears he will speak, and he will declare to you the things that are to come. He will glorify me for he will take what is mine and declare it to you" (16:13-14).

This also tells us for whom the Spirit is the Counselor and to whom the Spirit speaks. In the rest of the New Testament we are shown that the Spirit, like Christ, stands before the throne of God and pleads and intercedes for others. But the gospel of John does not see the need for an intercessor, since Jesus is in heaven where life has its source. It is the Spirit who speaks for Jesus in the world and is, so to speak, his successor and representative. The Spirit leads and directs his cause in the world. " . . . If I do not go away, the Counselor will not come to you; but if I go, I will send him to you. And when he comes, he will convince the world concerning sin and righteousness and judgment" (16:4ff.; see especially verses 7 and 8). Jesus also said, "He will bear witness to me" (see 15:26-27), i.e., against the world's hate. The thought here is that the disciples will experience rejection by their own people and thus from the synagogue. The charismatic events in the early church were a decisive issue for the synagogue. The gospel of John emphasizes the fact that God speaks to the synagogue through Jesus. The gospel declares to the Jews, who think and say they believe in God, that the true God is only present where the word of Jesus is spoken and heard. The Counselor witnesses to the identity of Jesus and says that God acts and speaks through him. Wherever the Word of God is heard, one's fate is already sealed.

The Spirit directs the word of Jesus not only to the world, but also to the Christian congregation. The Spirit is Jesus' representative to the faithful; it teaches the congregation and guides it into the whole truth. But although the word of Jesus is connected to the Spirit, and through the Spirit to the church, the church does not have the word at its disposal so that it has power over the word. The miracle of preaching is that the word of Jesus remains the tool of the Spirit. It is the Spirit which makes it possible for the words of Jesus to be repeated, applied, actualized, and interpreted in ever new situations. It is the Spirit which gives the words of Jesus continued relevance and eternal validity. Thus, the importance of Jesus for the world did not end with his death, but continues through the proclamation of the Word. It is Jesus' words which determine the fate of the world as well as our own fate, once and for all, and not vice versa.

By this time it should be apparent that the author of the gospel of John is a master of simplification. The Holy Spirit for him is nothing other than the continual proclamation of Jesus' words and the great mystery that these words determine the fate and destiny of mankind.

NINE

Something about Ourselves—
Those to Whom the
Gospel Is Addressed

Now that we have looked at several main thoughts in the
gospel, we may again raise the difficult question about the
historical situation in which the gospel came into being and
who the original readers of the gospel may have been. We
mentioned earlier that the gospel of John is a great riddle
for New Testament research. This is partly due to the fact
that we do not know who its original readers were.

What we propose in the following lines is only one of
many theories concerning the contemporary situation in
which the gospel of John was written, but it is not a usual
explanation.

The author of the gospel of John explains why he writes
his gospel (see 20:31): so that whoever reads his words may
believe that Jesus is the Messiah, the Son of God. The word
Messiah is not a name, but a title. Its use makes clear that
the title is important for those for whom the gospel is written. At the same time, we note that the gospel has a de-
cidedly polemical tone, often expressed in the insistence of
the author that what he writes is true (1:9; 6:32; 15:1; 17:3;
et al.). The word *true* in this context stands for that which
is real, final, and absolute in contrast to whatever is only

illusory and temporary. The word is sometimes directed against those who claim that what they represent is true (1:17).

The gospel's polemic is definitely directed against the Jews. Jesus has to contend against conflict and strife; it is the Jews who oppose him, as we shall see from several references. It is the signs Jesus performs which become the center of contention. In Chapter 5 we have the account of a healing at Bethesda. That the healing took place on the Sabbath leads to a discussion about the identity of Jesus. The miracle of the loaves takes place in the following chapter, which leads to the claim that Jesus is the bread of life. Chapter 9 tells us about the healing of the man born blind. This is the beginning of a long investigation by the Pharisees of the one who was healed, and of a debate about Jesus. Chapters 1–12 of the gospel are characterized by debate between Jesus and the Jewish people.

The opposition of the Jews to Jesus is presented much more systematically in John than in the other gospels. But only the Jews in general are referred to; they are not distinguished according to the various groups of Jews existing at the time of Jesus, for instance, the Pharisees, Sadducees, Herodians, Zealots, etc. The Fourth Gospel refers not to a conflict, from the past, but to one which it considers to be continually contemporary, as is particularly seen from 15:18 through 16:4. In the so-called farewell discourse (Chapters 14-17) Jesus broaches events to follow his death— his followers will be subject to hate, rejection, persecution, and death.

The conflict referred to is thus an ongoing conflict. The Jews form the one party in the conflict, and it is against them the gospel is directed. But they represent more than the Jews, for they arise as representatives of the world which God opposes (8:23,26; 10:36). It is precisely the chosen people who become the enemies of God. But what about the other party in the conflict? Are they possibly Christians of gentile origin who have come into conflict with Jewish Christians within the church? It may be that we are given a clue with the use of the Jewish title *Messiah*. This title would not be of any particular interest to Gentiles, and *Messiah* is not used elsewhere in the gospel of John except as a title. Thus, the author of the gospel shows that Jesus is the Messiah whom the Jews have awaited and looked for (1:20,41,45; 4:25,29; 7:26,27; 10:24; 11:27). That the thought pattern is Jewish becomes more obvious from these words spoken to Jesus, "Rabbi, you are the Son of God! You are the King of Israel!" (1:49; see also 18:28ff.). With the use of such language, the gospel of John is saying that Jesus is the Messiah promised to the Jews. But how do we then understand the anti-Jewish polemic of the gospel?

The events of the gospel revolve around the Jews. Jesus moves about only within Jewish territory. Gentiles appear only once (12:20ff.), and even then they are Greeks who have come to worship in Jerusalem. The gospel has no particular interest in non-Jews or in a mission to the Gentiles.

We also note that the term *Israelite* becomes a term of honor, as in the phrase, "an Israelite indeed, in whom is no guile" (1:47). The same is true of the term *rabbi*, or Jewish teacher (1:38). This too would seem to indicate a Jewish readership. This is reinforced still further when we discover the way in which the gospel makes use of the Scriptures—our Old Testament—and the emphasis it places upon the figure of Moses. John attempts to point to all that is positive between Moses and Jesus. We need look no further than this statement: "For the law was given through Moses; grace and truth came through Jesus Christ" (1:17). There is no attempt to discredit Moses, although he, unlike Jesus, is temporary. He points forward to the coming of Jesus. Thus, the events Moses depicts in the books of the Old Testament which tradition ascribes to his hand, point to Jesus. If one believes in Moses, he must also believe in Jesus (1:45; 5:45-46; 9:28-29). Moses, the very epitome of everything Jewish, was used by those who rejected Christ as an argument against the faith of the church, and the author of John seeks to do away with this argument. He shows that Moses does not represent a Jewish belief and thought which is contrary to Christianity. Moses represents the temporary and has himself pointed in his writings to the coming of Christ. Jesus is the very content of the Mosaic writings. Consequently, anyone who occupies himself with Moses must eventually accept Jesus.

This, too, indicates a Jewish readership. At the same time, the gospel hurls polemic against the Jews; but this is not strange, as we shall see. Before we clarify this matter, however, one thing more must be understood. The gospel of John shows us how Jesus' preaching splits the Jews (6:52; 7:12,40-44; 9:16; 10:19-20). At the same time he says that many Jews believed in Jesus (7:1; 8:30-31; 11:45,48-50; 12:42). Yet, it is shown that their faith is weak, and it is easy for them to backslide, usually the result of debates held with Jews who do not believe (7:31; 6:60ff.).

We are told in one statement that even Jewish leaders come to faith (12:42). This statement gives us an interesting additional clue to the environment and situation of the readers of the gospel. It is said about these leaders that they believed in Jesus but dared not confess their faith out of fear that they would be "put out of the synagogue." This phrase appears only here and in two other places in the gospel of John; it does not appear elsewhere in the New Testament and is not found in any Greek literature. It is translated literally as "expelled from the synagogue." It is used in the story of the healing of the man born blind. The reference is to an ordinance or ruling. The parents of the blind man dare say nothing to anyone about the healing, because they knew that anyone who confessed Jesus as the Messiah would be put out of the synagogue. Such a decree did not exist at the time of the actual healing. We know, too, that the early Christians continued to worship in the temple and the synagogues for a time, as is accurately reported in the book of Acts. The decree, to which John makes indirect reference in Chapter 9, came into effect sometime toward the end of the first century A.D., at any rate after A.D. 70. But the fact that the decree is referred to at all tells us something about the circumstances at the time the gospel of John was written. The situation is one which has arisen following the death of Jesus and, in fact, is the result of Jesus' death, as we see from 16:1-4. Here it is said that those who believe in Jesus *shall* be put out of the synagogue; they shall be put to death because the synagogue does not know God. Thus we see that Christians living when the gospel of John was being written were being forced out of the synagogue. The gospel asserts that the Jewish congregation has, by its rejection of Jesus and those who believe in him, also rejected God. In doing so, they have actually thrown God out of his own house. Their rejection has given Christian Jews cause for doubt and anxiety. As might be expected, they undergo an identity crisis. They have to fight against the argumentation which says that the Scriptures, the Law, Moses, and the prophets all speak against Jesus. The gospel is therefore written to a Jewish-Christian congregation for whom faith in Jesus as the Messiah is in danger of being lost. Or we could say in more contemporary sounding language, the message is directed to a congregation on the verge of becoming foreign to its own environment and traditions and must therefore struggle with its own identity.

It is against this background that the gospel of John becomes most comprehensible from beginning to end. The author stresses that no doubt must prevail that it is God himself who speaks and acts in Jesus Christ. It is major concern that sight of this truth not be lost, and therefore the gospel is a word of encouragement to Christian Jews in their hour of crisis. The blame for the strife is put where it belongs, namely, on those who do not believe that God speaks and acts in Jesus. The gospel affirms that God does just that; God's Word is to be found in the words of Jesus. The prologue presents Jesus as the divine Word through whom everything has been made (1:1ff.). Jesus also possesses divine glory (1:14), by which is revealed the nature and will of God. This is the assertion of a number of texts: "He who has seen me has seen the Father . . . " (14:9b); "No one has ever seen God; the only Son, who is in the bosom of the Father, he has made him known" (1:18); "I and the Father are one" (10:30); "Holy Father, keep them in thy name which thou hast given me, that they may be one, even as we are one" (17:11b). Such statements reveal the emphasis which is to be found throughout the gospel, namely, that Jesus has been sent by the Father and lives in direct fellowship with him.

Jesus' words and teachings also hold a central position in the gospel, in a double sense. On the one hand, it is stressed that Jesus' words come directly from God and can therefore only be understood as being the very words of God. As we have seen, the evangelist says that what Jesus says is what he himself has seen and heard from the Father. He has seen the Father (3:11; 8:26,38; 15:15; 17:18). God has told him what he is to say (12:49-50; 10:18). Jesus' words are not his own, but God's words (14:24). It may also be said that Jesus' words are spirit (6:63), which means they are words from God because God is spirit (4:24). The gospel uses these and many similar statements to emphasize the very main point that it is not Jesus alone who speaks, but God through Jesus. Thus, it is the God of Israel who speaks through Jesus' words.

The authority with which Jesus speaks to a Jewish setting can only be understood on the basis of our Old Testament. Biblical research does not overlook the fact that the gospel of John makes extensive use of the Old Testament, but it does overlook the fact that these Scriptures are often used in a unique way, at least in relation to other New Testament writings. The evangelist does not say that the Old Testament Scriptures are to be fulfilled by Jesus; he says rather that the Scriptures speak directly about Jesus. Thus, the Old Testament writers had Jesus in mind when they wrote. Messianic prophecies are therefore not to be fulfilled in Jesus, but address themselves to Jesus from the very beginning. It is asserted that Moses wrote about Jesus (5:46). Jesus said, "You search the scriptures, because you think that in them you have eternal life; and it is they that bear witness to me" (5:39). If the Jews had read and correctly understood what they read, they would have believed in Jesus. And now they stand accused by the very one whom they claim to be exclusively their own, Moses himself (5:45). The Scriptures cannot stand alone; they must point the reader or hearer away from themselves to Jesus. The Jews refuse to believe in Jesus because they refuse to believe what is written. They do not have a proper relationship even to their own sacred writings. They are unlike their father Abraham, who looked to the appearing of Jesus (8:56ff.); he is thus, unlike his descendants, a witness to Christ. When it is said that Abraham saw Jesus, the thought is, of course, that Jesus existed before his incarnation. It was therefore entirely possible for Abraham to have a vision of him. Finally, it is stated that the Old Testament prophet

Isaiah saw the glory of Jesus as he wrote (12:41). The reference here is to the vision described by Isaiah: "In the year that King Uzziah died, I saw the Lord sitting upon a throne, high and lifted up; and his train filled the temple" (Isa. 6:1). The gospel of John interprets the one sitting upon the throne as Jesus. This is done to counterattack the synagogue's rejection of Jesus. The evangelist supports his claim on the basis of Scripture. The Jews can therefore no longer use the Scriptures to support their rejection. The Scriptures witness to Jesus, and so do the Jewish fathers.

We shall look at one more characteristic of the gospel helpful for determining its background. We refer to the kind of dualism which we find in the gospel; i.e., humanity is separated into two groups which also existed before the coming of Christ. Those in the one group are of the truth and doers of the truth; they have their origin in God and belong to the Messiah's fold. Those in the other group are of untruth and the doers of evil; they belong to the world and have their origin in the devil (3:20,21; 8:23,44,47; 10:26,27; 17:6,9,14). When Christ comes, these two groups will be visibly separated in the judgment; it will be made evident at this time where each group belongs. For John, in a way the church has existed long before the coming of Christ, because to the church belong precisely those who are of the truth and who have been there long before Jesus. There is thus a form of dualism in this gospel, and because these two groups of people have existed side by side before Christ, it can also be understood as a form of predestination or predetermination.

This may seem extremely confusing and unclear unless seen against the actual background of the gospel, the Christian church and the Jewish synagogue. The two groups, described above, were not separated until the coming of Christ, at which time it became known to which side they belonged. They lived together as Israel, as the Jewish congregation. When the groups were separated from each other with the coming of Christ, there occurred a breaking away and separation from the synagogue. The group which became the church had its origins in the synagogue, but is now a separate entity. But it is the church which has inherited the rights and privileges of Israel. The gospel of John states clearly that it is now the Christians who have a claim to everything the Jews claim as their own: God, history, salvation, the Holy Scriptures. The Christians have always been God's people, while the unbelieving Jews have never been God's people. The old biblical religion and faith do not live in the synagogue, but in the congregation of God's Son.

TEN

Scholarship and the Gospel of John

What appears on the preceding pages of this book does not give any impression of the wide variety of opinions when it comes to interpreting the gospel of John. We cannot speak of any consensus.

Throughout the history of biblical hermeneutics we often see that a particular writing finds an interpreter who, in some way or another, unlocks some of its mysteries, not only for his contemporaries, but those in later generations as well. An example is Paul's letter to the Romans as it has been interpreted by Augustine and Luther. The same is true of a number of other New Testament writings, with the exception of the gospel of John. An examination of the literature dealing with this gospel leads us to observe that scholarship, to a certain extent, has had to grope in the dark, and that the mystery connected with the Fourth Gospel is far from being solved.

This may be an added incentive for those who might themselves wish to arrive at a solution of the problems. The bibliography and notes which follow are for the assistance mainly of those who wish to pursue the matter further. We have put heaviest emphasis on works of more recent scholarship, covering mainly the last 20 years or so. But we have also included a few older works, particularly those which have contributed to the debate by raising significant questions. Works which give us a general survey of scholarly research on John, including both earlier and more recent studies, are:

W. F. Howard, *The Fourth Gospel in Recent Criticism and Interpretation*, rev. by C. K. Barrett, London, 1955.

R. Kysar, *The Fourth Evangelist and His Gospel: An Examination of Contemporary Scholarship*, Minneapolis: Augsburg, 1975.

Works which investigate the *sources* utilized by the evangelist are numerous, with about as many opinions as there are scholars. Recent scholarship on the Gospel of John has been influenced more by R. Bultmann's commentary, *The Gospel of John*, than any other volume. This work was first published in German in 1941. Bultmann concluded that the author of John had made use of four sources:

1. A document describing the miracles of Jesus.

2. A revelatory document with discourses in which a redeemer figure speaks to the initiated.

3. A source containing an account of Jesus' suffering, death, and resurrection.

4. A number of minor sources of mixed content.

Bultmann asserts that the evangelist has incorporated aspects of these sources in his writing, but the final form of the gospel as we know it today is the result of the additions and changes made by a later editor, for whom it was necessary to fit the gospel to a more orthodox, churchly faith. The scholarly debate regarding these various sources is largely determined by one's position to Bultmann, and is built upon the foundation laid by him. A number of important contributions are:

H. Becker, *Die Reden des Johannesevangeliums und der Stil der gnostischen Offenbarungsreden*, Göttingen, 1956.

R. T. Fortna, *The Gospels of Signs: A Reconstruction of the Narrative Source Underlying the Fourth Gospel*, Cambridge, 1970.

W. Nicol, *The Semeia in the Fourth Gospel*, Leiden, 1972.

E. Ruckstuhl, *Die literarische Einheit des Johannesevangeliums*, Freiburg, 1951.

E. Schweizer, *Ego Eimi*, Göttingen, 1939.

H. Teeple, *The Literary Origin of the Gospel of John*, Evanston, Illinois: Religion and Ethics Institute, Inc., 1974.

To the question of sources utilized by the author of John must also be added another much debated question, namely, the use made by the Fourth Gospel of the other three, the so-called synoptic Gospels. There has been a tendency on the part of some to reject completely any literary dependency on the part of the evangelist upon any of these. On the other hand, there are those who believe that to some extent or another in the development of the Fourth Gospel there has been a dependency upon the other gospels. But the majority of scholars believe they are independent of each other.

J. A. Bailey, *The Traditions Common to the Gospels of Luke and John*, Leiden, 1963.

J. Blinzler, *Johannes und die Synoptiker*, Stuttgart 1965.

C. H. Dodd, *Historical Tradition in the Fourth Gospel*, Cambridge, 1963.

B. Noack, *Zur Johanneischen Tradition*, Copenhagen, 1954.

P. Gardner Smith, *Saint John and the Synoptic Gospels*, Cambridge, 1938.

Authorship of the gospel of John is still under consideration. There are many opinions, but the debate has generally followed the belief traceable back to the second century A.D., namely, that it is Jesus' own disciple John, the son of Zebedee, who has written the gospel. The clear tendency today has been to reject this. Some have believed John Mark, missionary, and for a time Paul's traveling companion, to be the author. The great majority, however, have suggested numerous authors who for us remain more or less anonymous.

B. Lindars, *The Gospel of John*, London, 1972.

Th. Lorenzen, *Der Lieblingsjünger im Johannesevangelium: Eine redaktionsgeschichtliche Studie*, Stuttgart, 1971.

J. Colson, *L'enigme du disciple que Jésus aimait*, Paris, 1969.

H. P. V. Nunn, *The Authorship of the Fourth Gospel*, Oxford, 1952.

R. Schnackenburg, *The Gospel According to St. John*, New York: Herder and Herder, 1968, vol. 1.

B. de Solages, "Jean, fils du Zébédéé et l'enigme du 'disciple que Jésus aimait,' " *Bulletin de Litteráture Ecclesiastique* 73, 1972, 41ff.

Tied up with the problem of sources and authorship is the study of composition and structure, i.e., how sources and traditions have been used. The following titles deal with this question:

R. E. Brown, *The Gospel According to John, I-II*, Garden City, N.Y.: Doubleday, 1966-1970.

G. H. C. Macgregor and A. Q. Morton, *The Structure of the Fourth Gospel*, Edinburgh, 1961.

D. M. Smith, *The Composition and Order of the Fourth Gospel*, New Haven: Yale University Press, 1965.

W. Wilkens, *Die Entstehungsgeschichte des vierten Evangeliums*, Zürich, 1958.

Many studies have attempted to determine the author's milieu, which for us is the *religious-historical setting*. The opinions form a broad spectrum, all the way from Hellenistic Gnosticism to one form or another of Judaism. Earlier scholarship has tended to place the gospel setting in a pre-Christian Gnosticism. There is a general consensus among modern day scholars that the gospel must be seen against a background of heterodoxical Judaism, even though the older view is not without its adherents. It is, of course, important in this connection to understand the relationship of the gospel to the Old Testament, which could give a clue concerning the possible Jewish setting.

W. Bauer, *Das Johannesevangelium*, 3d ed., Tübingen 1933.

O. Betz, *Der Paraklet*, Leiden, 1963.

R. Bultmann, *The Gospel of John*, translated from the 18th German edition, Philadelphia: Westminster, 1971.

F.-M. Braun, *Jean le Théologien II*, Paris, 1966.

C. H. Dodd, *The Interpretation of the Fourth Gospel*, Cambridge, 1953.

E. D. Freed, *Old Testament Quotations in the Gospel of John*, Leiden, 1965.

T. F. Glasson, *Moses in the Fourth Gospel*, London, 1963.

J. P. Miranda, *Der Vater, der mich gesandt hat*, Frankfurt, 1972.

W. A. Meeks, *The Prophet-King*, Leiden, 1967.

G. Reim, *Studien zum alttestamentlichen Hintergrund des Johannesevangeliums*, Cambridge, 1974.

L. Schottroff, *Der Glaubende und die feindliche Welt*, Neukirchen, 1970.

S. Schulz, *Das Evangelium nach Johannes*, Göttingen, 1972.

G. Stemberger, *la Symbolique du bien et du mal selon Saint Jean*, Paris, 1970.

What did the author understand to be his purpose in writing the gospel? What is the situation in which he finds himself? To whom is the gospel addressed? These problems are not unlike others which give the gospel its puzzling character. Scholars have viewed the gospel in such different ways: as a polemical statement against the disciples of John the Baptist; as a missionary document directed against the Jews; as a defensive apologetic directed against the synagogue; as an argument against the gnostics or Christian Docetists; and as a writing to give encouragement to Christians whether of Jewish or Gentile backgrounds. Today the tendency is to understand the purpose of the gospel in relation to a definite break with the Jewish synagogue, from which a number of those in the Christian congregation have come.

C. K. Barrett, *Das Johannesevangelium und die Juden*, Stuttgart, 1970.

K. Bornhauser, *Das Johannesevangelium eine Missionsschrift für Israel*, Gütersloh, 1928.

E. Grässer, "Die Antijüdische Polemik im Johannesevangelium," *New Testament Studies* 10, 1964-65, p. 74ff.

E. Hoskyns, *The Fourth Gospel*, London, 1940.

H. Leroy, *Rätzel und Missverständnis*, Bonn, 1968.

W. A. Meeks, *The Prophet-King*, Leiden, 1967.

J. Louis Martyn, *History and Theology in the Fourth Gospel*, New York: Harper and Row, 1968.

G. W. MacRae, "The Fourth Gospel and Religionsgeschichte," *Catholic Biblical Quarterly* 32, 1970, p. 17ff.

The literature we have thus far listed should serve to point out the most important element for understanding the gospel of John, namely, how the author himself interprets and understands the Christian message. What is the *understanding* and *theological perspective* of the author? Bultmann's major work, to which we have already made reference, is of primary importance here, not least with regard to the Christology and eschatological understanding of the author of John.

Bultmann has shown us how crucial the gospel's view of eschatology, i.e., the teachings about the end time, is to us for a proper understanding of the Fourth Gospel. For Bultmann, with some background in existentialist thought, the gospel of John understands that the last things and the end time do not belong to some future moment, but have already been ushered in with the coming of Christ and are experienced as the end time now by those who believe in him. Statements in the gospel reveal a dichotomy here, for the evangelist also adheres to a future day of judgment, but Bultmann believes these are later additions by the churchly editor who has desired to "fit" the author into a more churchly/orthodox theology. To this approach to the eschatological problem must also be added the relationship between the understanding of history and faith in the gospel.

J. Blank, *Krisis. Untersuchungen zur Johanneischen Christologie und Eschatologie*, Freiburg, 1964.

R. Bultmann, *The Gospel of John* (see above).

R. Bultmann, *Theology of the New Testament*, Translated from the German, New York: Scribners, 1951.

O. Cullmann, *Salvation in History*, Translated from the German, New York: Harper and Row, 1965.

N. A. Dahl, "The Johannine Church and History," *Current Issues in New Testament Interpretation*, W. Klassen and G. F. Snyder, N.Y., 1962, p. 124ff.

L. van Hartingsveld, *Die Eschatologie des Johannesevangeliums*, Assen, 1962.

Fr. Mussner, *The Historical Jesus in the Gospel of John*, London, 1967.

P. Ricca, *Die Eschatologie des vierten Evangeliums*, Zürich, 1966.

J. Riedl, *Das Heilswerk nach Johannes*, Freiburg, 1973.

H. Schlier, "Zur Christologie des Johannesevangeliums," *Das Ende der Zeit*, Freiburg, 1971, p. 85ff.

Another major theme in Johannine theology is the relationship between the *human* and the *divine* in the person of Jesus. This has its source mainly in the important prologue text of 1:14 which speaks about the Word made flesh ("became a human being" in the Today's English Version) but which also possesses divine glory (*doxa*). Bultmann understands this to be a paradoxical relationship in which the divine and the human belong together, but in such a way that the divine is present, though hidden, in Jesus' humanity. Post-Bultmann studies in this area have been greatly influenced by the provocative statements by E. Käsemann. The evangelist has to contend with a naive Docetism, therefore the Johannine Jesus is from beginning to end in the gospel a divine figure, whose divine glory does not suddenly disappear at any point in his life.

R. Bultmann, *Theology of the New Testament* (see above).

W. H. Cadman, *The Open Heaven: The Revelation of God in the Johannine Sayings of Jesus*, Oxford, 1969.

A. Feillet, *Le Mystere de l'amour divin dans la théologie johannique*, Paris, 1972.

K. Hacker, *Die Stiftung des Heils. Untersuchungen zur Struktur der johanneischen Theologie*, Stuttgart, 1972.

E. Haenchen, "Der Vater der mich gesandt hat," *New Testament Studies* 9, 1963, p. 21ff.

J. Kuhl, *Die Sendung Jesu und der Kirche nach dem Johannes-evangelium*, St. Augustin, 1967.

E. Käsemann, *The Testament of Jesus According to John 17*, Translated from the German, Philadelphia: Fortress Press, 1968.

L. Schottroff, *Der Glaubende und die feindliche Welt*, Neukirchen, 1970.

Concerning the Johannine understanding of *the church*, Bultmann asserts there is no particular ecclesiological (churchly) interest for the author of the Fourth Gospel. Related to this is how important the sacraments have been for the evangelist. Here, too, there is a wide spectrum of opinion. Some scholars maintain that the author is essentially antisacramentalist, while others maintain that he gives them a stronger position. Of importance here is how one views those passages in John where there can be no doubt that the sacraments are discussed in a positive manner. The question is, are these insertions made by someone who wanted to give a more orthodox twist to the theology of the gospel?

R. Bultmann (see works cited above).

P. Borgen, *Bread from Heaven*, Leiden, 1965.

N. A. Dahl (see above).

E. Käsemann, *The Testament of Jesus According to John 17* (see above).

H. Klos, *Die Sakramente im Johannesevangelium*, Stuttgart, 1970.

E. Lohse, "Wort und Sakrament im Johannesevangelium," *New Testament Studies* 7, 1960–61, p. 11ff.

W. Michaelis, *Die Sakramente im Johannesevangelium*, Bern, 1946.

P. Niewalda, *Sakramentsymbolik im Johannesevangelium*, Limburg, 1958.

E. Schweizer, *Gemeinde und Gemeindeordnung im Neuen Testament*, Zürich, 1959.

Related to the understanding of the church in the gospel of John is the presentation of the Spirit. As discussed earlier, this gospel has a very unique way of designating the Holy Spirit, and the ecstatic seems to be lacking entirely. The following works deal with the term *Counselor*, the Paraclete (Chapters 14–16), and the role this term plays in the gospel:

O. Betz, *Der Paraklet*, Leiden, 1963.

G. Bornkamm, "Der Paraklet im Johannesevangelium," *Festschrift für R. Bultmann*, Stuttgart, 1949, p. 12ff.

G. Johnston, *The Spirit-Paraclete in the Gospel of John*, Cambridge, 1971.

H. Schlier, "Der Heilige Geist als Interpret nach dem Johannesevangelium," *Int. Katholische Zeitschrift "Communio*," 2, 1973, p. 97ff.

There are also at hand an enormous number of commentaries which treat the gospel of John as a whole. R. Bultmann's commentary of 1941 is a work that continues to influence all other works of this type also. In addition to this major work, which will continue to be read for a long time to come, we list the following which, because of their varying points of view and scope, can supply the serious student who wishes to pursue the gospel independently with basic material:

C. K. Barrett, *The Gospel According to St. John*, 1955.

W. Bauer, *Das Johannesevangelium*, 3d ed., Tübingen, 1935.

Rudolf Bultmann, *The Gospel of John* (see above).

R. E. Brown, *The Gospel According to John*, *I-II* (see above).

E. Hoskyns, *The Fourth Gospel*, 2d ed., 1947.

M.-J. Lagrange, *Evangile selon Saint Jean*, Paris, 1925.

B. Lindars, *The Gospel of John*, London, 1972.

A. Loisy, *Le Quatrieme Evangile*, 2d ed., Paris, 1921.

A. Schlatter, *Der Evangelist Johannes*, 2d ed., Stuttgart, 1948.

R. Schnackenburg, *The Gospel According to St. John*, *I-III*, Translated from the German, New York: Seabury/Crossroad, 1968–82.

H. Strathmann, *Das Evangelium nach Johannes*, 7th ed., Göttingen 1954.